SUNDAY PASTA

A Year Around the Table with Family and Friends

EDWIN GARRUBBO

www.Garrubbo.com

Copyright © 2014 by Edwin Garrubbo.

All rights reserved. No portion of this book may be reproduced—mechanically, electronically, or by any other means, including photocopying—without the written permission of the publisher.

Published in the United States by Garrubbo Communications, LLC.

www.Garrubbo.com

Sunday Pasta® and Garrubbo® are registered trademarks of Garrubbo Communications, LLC.

Library of Congress Cataloging-in Publication date is available upon request.

ISBN 978-0-9890291-0-0

eISBN 978-0-9890291-1-7

Printed in China by Everbest Printing (Guangzhou) Co Ltd.

Book Design by Davide Carbone

Cover Design by Leah Lococo

Photography by Fabio Paparelli

10 9 8 7 6 5 4 3 2 1

First Edition

"Life is a combination of magic and pasta."
—Federico Fellini

ACKNOWLEDGMENTS

I would like to thank all the people who helped bring this book from idea to life. There are so many friends who have commented and contributed over the years. Those who have contributed to research, editing, and writing: Susan Simon, Emily Mikesell, Maggie O'Connor, Caroline Sherman, Mary Bing, Chris Galiardo, Christy Canterbury, Donna Picchiochi, Patricia Bazan Garrubbo. On the creative and design side: Davide Carbone, Leah Lococo, Stasia Blanco. Photography: Fabio Paparelli, Jay Joongyeol Ahn; Food Styling: Diane Vezza, Steve Corrado. Production and Printing: Jason Makowski, Gabriel Stuart. To the chefs and cooks who have contributed recipes or inspirations over the years, notably, Mamma, Chris Nalty, Vito Gnazzo, Cinzia Gaglio, Dean Caselnova, Angelo Pumilio, and the Menarosti family. And, in the interior cover photographs: Richard and Nancy Caccappolo; Eva, Chris, and Henry Caputo; Davide, Elda, and Ulisse Carbone; Philip, Dante, Damian, and Philly Jr. Garrubbo.

And of course, to my family, living and departed, who have shared recipes and cooked and eaten so many *Sunday Pasta* dinners with me.

A special thanks to my talented and *meravigliosa* wife Patricia, art director for the book, and to my children Sebastian and Veronica, who have been forced to eat a different delicious pasta dish each week for the past 5 years, even though all they really wanted to eat was more *spaghetti alla carbonara*.

For my father,
Mario Vittorio Orlando Garrubbo, 1941–2002.

What a guy.

CONTENTS

Why Sunday Pasta? 9

Inside Sunday Pasta 11

In Cucina *In the Kitchen* 12

    Protection of Origin 12
    Food Classification System 13
    Wine Classification System 13
    Formaggio *Cheese* 14
    Salumi *Cured Meats* 16
    Verdure *Vegetables* 17
    Frutta, Noci, e Miscellanea
        Fruits, Nuts, and Miscellany 20

PASTA BASICS 23

    A Brief History of Pasta 24
    Methods of preparation 25
    Cooking Pasta 27
    THE DO'S and DON'TS of PASTA 27
    Basic Pasta Recipe 28
    Salsa di Pomodoro
        Tomato Sauce 29
    Penne al Sugo di Pomodoro
        Penne with Tomato Sauce 30

SPRING RECIPES 33

    Ravioli di Spinaci al Burro e Salvia
        Spinach Ravioli with Butter and Sage ... 34
    Rigatoni alla Gricia
        Rigatoni with Pancetta and Onion 36
    Fusilli con Tonno e Pomodorini
        Fusilli with Tuna and Cherry Tomatoes ... 38
    Capricci Primavera (all'Ortolano)
        Capricci with Garden Vegetables 40

Tagliatelle alla Bolognese
    Tagliatelle with Meat Sauce 42
Calamarata con Gamberi e Asparagi
    Calamarata with Shrimp and Asparagus ... 44
Penne al Pistacchio
    Penne with Pistachios 46
Paglia e Fieno
    Tagliatelle with Prosciutto, Cream, and Peas ... 48
Spaghetti ai Carciofi
    Spaghetti with Artichokes 50
Bucatini con le Sarde
    Bucatini with Sardines 52
Spaghetti Aglio Olio e Peperoncino
    Spaghetti with Garlic, Chili Peppers, and Olive Oil ... 54
Orecchiette con Rapini e Salsiccia
    Orecchiette with Broccoli Rabe and Sausage ... 56
Tortellini alla Panna con Piselli
    Tortellini with Cream and Peas 58

SUMMER RECIPES 61

Spaghetti con le Vongole
    Spaghetti with Clams 62
Cavatappi con Rucola e Ricotta
    Cavatappi with Arugula and Ricotta 64
Spaghetti con Pomodoro e Basilico
    Spaghetti with Tomato and Basil 66
Trofie al Pesto Genovese
    Trofie with Basil Pesto 68
Mezza Rigatoni con Zucchine
    Mezza Rigatoni with Zucchini 70
Paccheri con Pesce Spada
    Paccheri with Swordfish 72
Linguine al Limone
    Linguine with Lemon 74
Pappardelle al Prosciutto
    Pappardelle with Prosciutto 76
Fusilli alla Checca
    Fusilli with Tomato and Mozzarella 78

Rigatoni alla Norma
Rigatoni with Eggplant 80

Gnudi di Spinaci e Ricotta
Spinach and Ricotta Gnudi 82

Tagliatelle con Radicchio e Speck
Tagliatelle with Radicchio and Speck 84

Bucatini Cacio e Pepe
Bucatini with Cheese and Black Pepper 86

FALL RECIPES 89

Paccheri con Salsiccia, Zucchine e Burrata
Paccheri with Sausage, Zucchini, and Burrata 90

Orecchiette con Ceci
Orecchiette with Chickpeas 92

Pennone al Gorgonzola
Pennone with Gorganzola 94

Spaghetti al Finocchio
Spaghetti with Fennel 96

Cavatelli con Broccoli
Cavatelli with Broccoli 98

Penne Integrale con Cavolini di Bruxelles
Whole Wheat Penne with Brussels Sprouts 100

Penne con Peperoni Arrosto
Penne with Roasted Red Peppers 102

Fusilli con Funghi, Pancetta e Pinoli
Fusilli with Mushrooms, Pancetta, and Pine Nuts 104

Conchiglie con Fagioli Rossi
Conchiglie with Red Beans 106

Fettuccine con Salsa di Noci
Fettucine with Walnut Sauce 108

Lasagna ai Funghi e Tartufi
Lasagna with Mushrooms and Truffles 110

Manicotti con Salsa di Pomodoro
Manicotti with Tomato Sauce 112

Rigatoni con le Polpettine
Rigatoni with Meatballs 114

WINTER RECIPES 117

Cavatelli con Ragù alla Napoletana
Cavatelli with Gravy and Braciola 118

Tagliatelle ai Funghi Porcini
Tagliatelle with Porcini Mushrooms 120

Strangozzi con le Capesante
Strangozzi with Scallops 122

Lasagna alla Bolognese
Lasagna with Meat Sauce 124

Pennone con Cavolfiore al Forno
Baked Pennone with Cauliflower 126

Timpano Pantheon
Meat and Pasta Pie 128

Spaghetti alla Carbonara
Spaghetti with Pancetta and Eggs 130

Pasta e Fagioli
Pasta and Beans 132

Spaghetti alla Puttanesca
Spaghetti with Olives, Capers, and Anchovies 134

Ziti al Forno
Baked Ziti 136

Spaghetti con Bottarga
Spaghetti with Fish Roe 138

Fusilli con Broccoli, Acciughe e Pinoli
Fusilli with Broccoli, Anchovies, and Pine Nuts 140

Bucatini all'Amatriciana
Bucatini with Pancetta, Tomato, and Onion 142

Risotto Basics 145

About Risotto 145

Risotto alla Milanese due Modi
Risotto Milanese Two Ways 146

Tabella della Pasta *Table of Pasta* **149**

Glossario *Glossary* **152**

Indice *Index* **157**

WHY SUNDAY PASTA?

ITALIAN FOOD HAS ALWAYS BEEN A CENTRAL PART OF MY LIFE. As a child, Sunday afternoons were spent at my grandparents' homes gathering with family and friends after church. Everything revolved around the meal: long antipasto courses, followed by pasta and meat and vegetables. Food was the magnet that drew us all together.

And, the food was delicious. My maternal mother, Mary Ciccone, made the best *ragú napoletano* and meatballs I've ever tasted. Anywhere. She passed this legacy on to my mother, Rosemary, who taught me to cook at a young age. My father, Mario, taught me to be critical about Italian food, to seek excellence and authenticity. His proud Sicilian mother Virginia Garrubbo lived to cook and, after 60 years of the craft, could rival any chef in anything Italian, from any region, appetizer to pastry. At restaurants, all eyes were upon her as we awaited her critical judgment of the food. I am lucky to have been raised in a delightful vortex of Italian comfort food.

I met some colorful characters during those meals, from doctors and lawyers to tailors and barbers, mostly Italian immigrants. I remember the laughing and arguing—and the decibel level—like it was yesterday. More than anything, I remember these slow-paced and conversational dinners as a weekly ritual that defines what family means to me.

Nowadays, it seems we are in constant motion, with every moment of the day compulsively planned. We schedule ourselves and our kids beyond capacity. We want more, and we want it faster. But in so doing, we have created a culture of stress and immediacy without reflection.

And so, a few years back, sparked by the death of my father, I decided that I wanted to do my small part to remind us all to "stop and smell the basil." To me, the answer was obvious: PASTA. Why Pasta? Because pasta is the food of kings and paupers: it is affordable, versatile, and easy to prepare, and fun to share. Well prepared pasta dishes include fresh, local, seasonal vegetables, dairy, meats and seafood, which in turn support healthy eating, the environment, the community and local food sourcing. These concepts seem trendy now, but are actually the result of the 3,000 years of evolution in Italian cooking. It is all right here, right now, right under our noses! All we need to do is slow down long enough to enjoy it.

I created a website, *The Garrubbo Guide,* and a blog, *Sunday Pasta,* to preserve and promote authentic Italian cooking and its many benefits. Every Sunday during the past five years, I have prepared a different pasta recipe for family and friends. Along with the recipe, I've included a wine pairing, some history about the ingredients, and a few personal musings. I call it Sunday Pasta because those two words capture the spirit of the idyllic family dinners that I remember so fondly. They say it all.

Sunday Pasta is a simple yet powerful idea: one delicious, nutritious meal per week, prepared with care and shared with those we love, will help all of us to enjoy the simple pleasures of life. In turn, it will inspire us to appreciate all the links in the chain, from plants to animals to people, who make our abundant foods available to us. So grab family and friends and start your very own *Sunday Pasta* tradition. It's easy. It's fun. It's delicious.

Buon Appetito!

Edwin Garrubbo

INSIDE SUNDAY PASTA

THIS BOOK CONTAINS JUST 54 RECIPES, MANY OF WHICH WOULD BE CONSIDERED WIDELY POPULAR IN ITALY. I have endeavored to provide only authentic Italian recipes, since my goal is to promote authenticity, and to highlight the Italian way of eating pasta. Many recipes come from my grandmothers, while others are from the Italian chefs and restaurants around Italy and the world that further inspire my love of Italian food. As a suggestion, the book offers one recipe for each week of the year, arranged chronologically, with consideration for the season, weather, and local ingredients. Of course, you can eat any of them at any time of year. They are generally quick and easy to prepare, and almost all allow for substitutions. If I can make them, anyone can, so try them all.

Each recipe is accompanied by a wine pairing—a short paragraph that provides the basic information you need to find the right wine for your pasta dish. The pairings were written by Christy Canterbury, MW, one of the 32 Masters of Wine in the United States, and an expert in Italian wines. Of course, wines from other parts of the world will do, but, understandably, I wanted an Italian focus. Also, in Italy, perhaps more than anywhere else, wine and food go hand in hand as part of the same culinary experience. We have endeavored to make the suggestions accessible to everyone, regardless of geographic location. Keep in mind, it is more important to note the qualities of the wines that match the ingredients of the dish rather than the exact wine mentioned.

The photographs were taken by Fabio Paparelli, a fashion photographer from Rome, now based in New York City. For many years, he owned a wine shop on Via Giulia in Rome, so he knows his wine, his art, and his Italian food. His background is a perfect fit as his beautiful work here attests.

In the *In Cucina* (In the Kitchen) section, I have included some interesting information about many of the key ingredients used in this book which are common in Italian cuisine, and often paired with pasta. Knowing your ingredients is an important part of learning to cook.

At the back of the book, there is a table of pastas, glossary, and index. With over 500 shapes and sizes of pasta in Italy, many of which have several names in different regions or dialects, I have tried to provide the basic information for making or buying the right pasta. While certain sauces are more appropriate for certain types of pastas, feel free to substitute within the same classifications. For example, if a recipe calls for penne, feel free to use another short, tubular pasta in its place. As a rule of thumb, light sauces are better with thinner, lighter pastas, and vice versa. Although the pasta ingredients may be the same, the shapes and sizes make the pasta taste different.

You will also find a *lagniappe*. In New Orleans, where I once lived, *lagniappe* means "a little something extra," like the 13th donut the baker gives you when you buy a dozen. Thus, I've included one recipe for risotto in this pasta book, that of the classic Risotto Alla Milanese. I love risotto and often prepare it. It can be as diverse as pasta when combined with all of the meats, vegetables, cheeses, and seafood that can accompany pasta. But with this book's narrow focus, there is only space for what you need to get started with risotto. You will find more risotto recipes in Sunday Pasta II!

This book is meant to be an extension of the much more elaborate website dedicated to preserving and promoting *la cucina Italiana*. For hundreds more recipes and in-depth wine pairings, and even more information about Italian food, please visit *The Garrubbo Guide* at www.Garrubbo.com.

IN CUCINA

In the Kitchen

The genius of Italian cooking lies in its simplicity. After all the years I've spent *in cucina*, I'm still amazed at how so few ingredients can produce such delicious meals. Perhaps the most delicious! In fact, though I've never counted, I've got this theory that I could live the rest of my life on only 100 ingredients. Since there are certain ingredients that make regular appearances in every Italian kitchen, as well as this book, I think it is important to understand a little bit about them. I've organized them by category: Formaggio (Cheese); Salumi (Cured Meat); Verdure (Vegetables); and Frutta, Noci, e Miscellanea. (Fruits, Nuts, and Miscellany).

Protection of Origin

Because Italian cuisine relies so on so few ingredients, Italians take the quality and authenticity of these ingredients to heart. For example, using an imitation "Parmesan" cheese rather than the genuine article could be worse than using none at all. Because the Italian government (in conjunction with the European Union) wants to protect the integrity of the foods for which Italy is famous, it has created a system by which it registers and protects certain culturally significant foods (and thereby the livelihoods of their producers).

As you will see, many recipes here call for foods that have been protected under this system. Some, like Prosciutto di Parma, can easily be found just about anywhere. Others may not be available, depending on popularity and ease of transport. As a rule, use the authentic ingredients when possible. If not, use the freshest substitutions you can find. (But I will personally guarantee that once you taste the genuine article, you will never go back.)

The Italian government created a similar system to protect and classify wines. For sure, there are many delicious Italian table wines, but the protected varieties are easier to trust when deciding what to buy.

Food Classification System

DOP—Denominazione di Origine Protetta—**Denomination of Protected Origin**

The DOP seal identifies a product whose entire production (from raw material to finished product) is geographically limited to a specific area.

IGP—Indicazione Geografica Protetta—**Protected Geographic Indication**

Somewhat laxer than the DOP seal, IGP requires at least one stage of production to happen in a specific area. IGP products can be tied to their areas of origin by an ingredient, a specific characteristic, or by reputation.

STG—Specialita' Tradizionale Garantita—**Guaranteed Traditional Specialty**

This is the most recent of the guarantee seals, implemented in 2006, and the only one not directly tied to a specific area. Its goal is to preserve and promote food products whose production follows traditional methods or recipes.

Wine Classification System

Vino Da Tavola—Table Wine, not falling within the confines of other denominations.

IGT—*Indicazione di Geografica Tipica*—**Indication of Typical Geography**—Defines where the wine is produced.

DOC—*Denominazione di Origine Controllata*—**Denomination of Controlled Origin**—Defines where the grapes are grown and how the wine is produced.

DOCG—*Denominazione di Origine Controllata e Garantita*—**(Guaranteed)**—Adds a guarantee of quality in addition to the above.

FORMAGGIO
Cheese

Burrata. This cow's milk cheese, originally from Puglia, is essentially mozzarella with a creamy filling that gives the cheese its name, "buttered." The outer layer of the cheese is stretched more than regular mozzarella, making its texture smoother. Shaped into an envelope, the center is left hollow, then filled with cream made from the whey mixed with strings of mozzarella. As the center portion ferments slightly inside its mozzarella cave, its taste becomes more complex.

Fontina. This is a mountain cheese from a region so close to Switzerland that it makes its own version of fondue, *fonduta*. Possibly named for a cheese-making family, a nearby town—Fontinaz, or the mountain, Fontin; Fontina D'Aosta is one of Italy's best-known cheeses, with documentation dating production back to the 18th century. It is firm but not hard, with a rind that is repeatedly washed until it acquires a characteristic, deep yellow/butterscotch brown color. Because Fontina D'Aosta must be made from the raw cow's milk of a single milking, it is made twice a day. It has a rich, complex flavor and yes, melts beautifully.

Gorgonzola. Gorgonzola is Italy's definitive blue, described as *erborinato* or "parsley-colored" in the dialect of Lombardy. *Erborinatura* is the method used to make blue cheese blue, or bluish green. Historically, mold in the caves where the cheese was aged eventually seeped into the cheese, giving it wonderful flavor. Today, gorgonzola wheels are pierced with stainless steel or copper needles to implant the necessary spores. Gorgonzola DOP encompasses two delicious cheeses with different tastes and textures. *Cremificato* is an oozy, silky, pungent cheese with dots of mold rather than actual veining. *Piccante* or mountain variety is creamy but in a crumbly way, with definite veining and a brighter tang. A third variety, *dolce* is softer and made for export.

Grana Padano. Literally, a "granular" cheese "of the Po Valley"; Grana Padano DOP is a cousin of Parmigiano Reggiano. It is a very hard cheese, suitable for grating, aged a maximum of 36 months, is made from part-skim cow's milk and has a gentle, nutty taste. Recent additions to the marketing of Grana Padano are labels stating levels of aging, such as "oltre 16 mesi" (more than 16 months) and "riserva" (reserve).

Mascarpone. Used in tiramisu, this rich cow's milk cream cheese is native to the Lombardy region. Italian cheese-makers drain the moisture from heavy cream with a finely woven cloth and a small amount of citric acid. After draining, a smooth, slightly sweet and fresh cheese remains.

Mozzarella. Mozzarella is a *pasta filata*, pulled or spun cheese, that is torn, *mozzare*, during the trickiest part of its preparation, hence the name. It has been made in Italy since the 2nd Century A.D. The brightest star in the mozzarella constellation is *Bufala Mozzarella di Compana* DOP, made with buffalo milk, originally produced by monks in the hills outside Salerno. It is the cheese of choice for authentic Neapolitan pizza. Also, as opposed to its cow's milk counterpart, mozzarella di bufala gets softer instead of stiffer as it loses freshness. All fresh mozzarella is smooth on the outside of its shaped ball (full-size or in bite-size *bocconcini*—"little mouthfuls" or *ciliegini*—"little cherries") and slightly elastic on the inside.

Parmigiano Reggiano. A hard, pressed cheese, or *formaggio presato,* made from a combination of skimmed and whole cow's milk; Parmigiano Reggiano is brined for three weeks and aged for at least a year—being periodically brushed and oiled for the duration. By that time, the 80 pound wheels have acquired a rock-hard rind and a nutty, crumbly, complex, delicious interior, suitable for grating, but wonderful as a table cheese. It is easy to recognize Parmigiano Reggiano DOP both from of its depth of flavor and because the rind is stamped with its name.

Pecorino. Pecorino is a generic term, meaning sheep cheese, or literally, little sheep cheese. There are quite a few representations of Pecorino, but the defining member of the family is Pecorino Romano; a delicious, firm table cheese at five months of age, suitable for grating after eight. Part of Roman soldiers' daily rations, its heritage is alive and well today. Although its name defines its traditional area of production, much of the DOP Pecorino Romano made today is made in Sardegna. And so, a class distinction is made: Pecorino Romano produced in the area surrounding Rome is labeled "Genuino". There is also a DOP Pecorino Sardo, but it is a semi-hard cheese that is aged for only a month or so.

Provolone. An ancient cheese, originally made in the Sorrentine peninsula, the name is taken from *prova* or *provala* which describe cheese samples. (And there are several Italian cheese varieties with prova or provala in their names.) Provolone [is made like mozzarella and aged like caciocavallo (a firm cheese), so it] starts with an elastic texture and becomes harder and drier over time.

Ricotta. In strict terms, ricotta is not cheese, but rather a dairy product, made when the whey is "re-cooked" and gives up its proteins. The formed solids are then drained, traditionally, in a basket, leaving a woven pattern. There are many varieties of ricotta: dry-salted or *salata*, *affumicata* (smoked), *Mustia and al Fumo di Ginepro* (smoked specifically by a juniper fire), *gentile* (creamy*)* and *forte* (tangy*).* Considerably drier than our US counterpart, some ricottas are very close in taste and texture to feta, but fresh ricotta in Italy is far creamier than anything in a U.S. supermarket.

Ricotta Salata. Native to the hot and dry climate of Sicily, this variation of Ricotta is white and firm with no rind. Its lightly salted sheep's milk curds are pressed and dried prior to aging for at least three months. The mild flavor of this cheese is somewhat nutty, with plenty of sweetness. Ricotta Salata is an excellent grating cheese for use on pasta and salads.

SALUMI
Cured Meats

Affettati is a general term, literally "sliced," but best translated in English as "cold cuts." In Italy, *affettati* are often sold in a specialized store called a *Salumeria*, so *affettati* can also be called *salumi*. *Insaccati*, a sub-category of *salumi*, include *salciccia* (fresh or dried sausages) as well as ground meats which are then encased, like *salame* or *soppresata*. *Affettati* would also include cured meats made from whole cuts like *prosciutto* and *coppa*. (Note: *salami* is the plural of salame, but Americans generally use this word to refer to the *salame* from Genoa.)

Guanciale. Cured pig's cheek or jowl, from *guancia*, cheek and *guanciale*, pillow. Richer than pancetta, guanciale is often produced in central Italy, most famously in Lazio, where it is the star ingredient in local versions of *pasta all'amatriciana, gricia, or carbonara.*

Pancetta. Italian bacon. This salt-cured pork belly is seasoned with nutmeg, pepper, fennel, dried, ground hot peppers, and garlic. It is dried for three months and served thinly sliced or chopped for pasta sauces or vegetables, often used as a less fatty alternative to guanciale.

Prosciutto. There is probably a prosciutto variety for every village in Italy. A master *salumiere* hand-trims and inspects each prosciutto ham. An intensive curing process includes rubbing and salting by hand, followed by long periods of air-drying. It is always served thinly sliced. The name describes the meat's journey—*prosciugare*, to drain away or dry up. Two of the most famous DOP versions are **Prosciutto di Parma** and **Prosciutto di San Daniele.**

Salsiccia. Sausage. "Insaccato di carne," or encased meat, dates back to Roman times, when it was first stuffed in pig intestines. Each region of Italy has its own variation of ingredients. The sausage recommended in this book is either "sweet" or "mild," but spicy, fennel, or other flavored Italian variety can be substituted.

Speck. This northern Italian relative of prosciutto is made by aging, salting, seasoning and cold-smoking a ham in the fresh air of Südtirol. *Speck dell'Alto Adige IGP* is known for its strong, pronounced aroma and unique, distinct flavor—the result of seasonings including juniper berry, pimento, black pepper and garlic. It has been made since the 1300s.

VERDURE
Vegetables

Aglio (Garlic). This member of the lily family has been in use in Italy since ancient times, but came from central Asia. It has been prized for centuries for its medicinal properties: strengthening the immune system, lowering blood pressure and acting as an antibacterial, to name a few. Perhaps more popular in the South, garlic is often used to flavor olive oil, and then removed from the pan before other ingredients are added.

Asparagi (Asparagus). A member of the lily family, cultivated asparagus is an Italian native, grows throughout the country and has been one of Italy's most popular vegetables since the Greeks and Romans enjoyed it. The name comes from the Greek *asparagos* and the Persian *asparag* meaning pertaining to growth: shoot, sprout, swollen. Asparagus grow in green, white and purple varieties, each having a slightly different flavor.

Basilico (Basil). Liguria is the land of basil and is, of course, the birthplace of *pesto genovese*, which is popular the world over. It is no surprise then, that the only protected variety is Basilico Genovese DOP. In terms of preparation some authorities preach a strict doctrine of tearing rather than cutting. More important, though, is maintaining temperature; if basil heats up, say, from banging up against a dull food processor blade, it will become bitter.

Broccoli. Broccoli is a cruciferous vegetable and member of the cabbage family. It is a result of careful breeding of cultivated leafy cole crops in the Northern Mediterranean in about the 6th century BC. The word broccoli, from the Italian plural of *broccolo* refers to "the flowering top of a cabbage." Since Roman Times, broccoli has been considered a uniquely valuable food among Italians.

Cavolfiore (Cauliflower). In the same family as broccoli, cauliflower has been eaten in Italy since the 16th Century. Originally regarded as a delicacy, cauliflower is now grown in Italy in white (Romanesco), green, purple, brown, and yellow cultivars. It is high in fiber, folate and vitamin C.

Cavolini (Cavoletti) di Bruxelles (Brussels Sprouts). A member of the cabbage family (along with broccoli, kale, collard greens), these sprouts were probably grown during the 13th century in what is now Brussels, Belgium, although their predecessors were likely cultivated in Ancient Rome. The edible buds grow on a large stalk, each producing 2–3 pounds of sprouts. Harvest season is September to March, which makes them a great fall and winter ingredient.

Carciofi (Artichokes). The globe artichoke is widely popular in Italy, especially in Rome. The edible portion of the plant consists of the flower buds before the flowers come into bloom. The uncultivated or wild variety of the species is called a cardoon. It is a perennial native to the Mediterranean region. While there are several types of artichokes available in Roman markets, the Romanesco is the only traditional choice for *Carciofi alla Giudia*.

Cipolla (Onion). A member of the lily family, Italians have grown onions since antiquity. Cipolle and cipollotte have at various times, been noted as improving health and/or libido. As a crop, they were a staple of peasant cuisine, eaten on or with bread. And they are one of the parts of *soffritto*, a combination of chopped onion, carrot and celery, sautéed and used as a base for many dishes.

Fagioli e Legumi (Beans and Legumes). Italian beans are harvested in the summer months. Markets are usually stocked by June and one can expect to find the cannellini and borlotti varieties all over Italy. Cannellini are small and white with a light flavor while borlotti are large ivory-colored beans with red streaks. Borlotti are known for their robust flavor. Tuscans in particular, are known for their love of beans, perhaps once for their value as a low-cost meat substitute, but now just as much in appreciation of their versatility.

Finocchio (Fennel). Finocchio is the bulbous plant. **Finochietto Selvatico (Wild Fennel: plant, seeds and pollen).** Fennel is both an herb and a spice. The slightly more bitter wild variety grows in central Italy. Its swollen, bulb-like stem can be eaten raw or cooked. Its flavorful and aromatic leaves and seeds can be dried and used as an herb and spice (although it is sometimes incorrectly called "anise.") Its medicinal qualities are also legendary, helping with high blood pressure, glaucoma, and intestinal distress.

Melanzane (Eggplant). Eggplant is one of the most popular foods in southern Italy. This vegetable ranges greatly in shape and size, from spherical and tiny to cylindrical and massive. It was once believed that consuming eggplants resulted in insanity and loose morals. A distinguishing characteristic of eggplant is its purple color, but this vegetable can be yellow or white as well. It cannot be eaten raw since it contains a toxin called solanine. It is important to salt eggplant before cooking because they tend to be very watery. Smaller sized eggplants are typically much less bitter than their larger counterparts.

Origano (Oregano). From the Greek word meaning "joy of the mountains," oregano makes a popular addition to many Italian preparations. It is used more in southern Italian cooking. Oregano is also an important medicinal herb. Slightly bitter and pungent, oregano is probably the only herb which is better dried than fresh and is usually sold that way.

Peperoncino (Chili Pepper). While pepper (black or white pepper) is definitely a fixture on Italian tables, peperoncino is much more identified with the country's southern regions. In Basilicata, the "little devil" diavolicchio, as it's called there, is the most widely used spice by far. Other regions also have their own names for this devilish spice. In Calabria, it is *peparuolo*, in Sicily, *pipi rossi*. Although the peppers may be used fresh, they are more likely to be dried and crushed into flakes for seasoning.

Peperoni (Bell Peppers). One of the few crops brought to Italy from the Americas by Columbus which was immediately embraced by the Italian people, peperoni or bell peppers now grow all over Italy. A young pepper will always start green, turning yellow, purple, or red with age, though some varieties remain green.

Piselli (Peas). Peas are one of the world's oldest foods, but the idea of eating fresh immature green peas was an Italian innovation. Peas are widespread in Italy, as either a main ingredient or a sweet addition to many recipes.

Pomodori (Tomatoes). The first tomatoes to appear in Italy were from South America and were yellow in color, which sparked the name pomodoro, or "golden apple." There are many varieties of tomato, each used for culinary purposes fitting to its particular set of characteristics. In Italy, there are two main classes of tomato; pomodori insalatari (used in salads), and pomodori da salsa (used for sauces and cooking). Pomodori insalatari are usually not completely ripened therefore streaks of green can be found throughout the firm fruit. Pomodori da salsa is red, slightly sweet, and rich in flavor. The majority of tomatoes grown in Italy come from Campania and Puglia, the most famous being the DOP San Marzano. It is a good idea to always have a few cans of San Marzano, whole peeled tomatoes with basil, in the cupboard.

Porcini (Mushrooms). The meaty mushroom works well in a variety of dishes ranging from grilled steaks to light soups and stews. Many Italian sauces contain porcini, as well. The white-stalked brown-capped mushroom is most commonly found growing underneath chestnut trees in Italian forests. Porcini are always better fresh, but they can be dried for later use.

Prezzemolo (Parsley). Flat-leaf parsley (or Italian parsley) is one of the most widely used herbs in Italy, beloved by the ancient Romans and seemingly everyone in Italy since then. It is also soothing to the stomach, provides relief from kidney stones, and was once thought to reverse the effects of poison.

Rapini (Broccoli Rabe). The edible parts of this popular cruciferous vegetable are the leaves, buds, and stems. The buds somewhat resemble broccoli, but do not form a large head. It is known for its slightly bitter taste, and is particularly associated with southern Italian cooking, especially in Campania, Puglia, and Lazio. In Italian, it is called *cime di rapa* (literally meaning "turnip tops"), *rapi*, or *rapini*; in Naples it is known as *friarielli* and sometimes *broccoli di rapa*; in Rome *broccoletti*.

Rosmarino (Rosemary). Rosemary loves to grow on the coast, hence its name, meaning "dew of the sea." It has grown in Italy for millennia, specifically in its dry scrublands, with evidence of the Etruscans in Tuscany using it in their cuisine and burial rites. It has a history of soothing the stomach and stimulating the memory. Its leaves look like pine needles and it does have an evergreen appearance and related scent.

Salvia (Sage). With its root in the Latin for health and healing, it is no surprise that sage was a primary medicinal herb before it became one of Italy's most beloved kitchen denizens. It is often paired with butter and served over ravioli in Northern Italy.

Radicchio. There are literally hundreds of different kinds of leafy greens, both cultivated and wild, growing in Italy. Radicchio is mentioned in the ancient texts of both nobles and monks and was thought to have had a medicinal quality, serving as a blood purifier or analgesic. Today, radicchio enjoys great popularity and has three protected varieties, including the famous long-leaf variety from Treviso and the more spherical variety from Trentino.

Spinaci (Spinach and Chard). Spinach and chard are both popular whether lightly cooked or served raw in a salad. *Erbette* is young chard, which is small, b*ietole* is larger, older chard, and *coste* (the ribs) are the largest (and are usually cooked separately from the leaves). Caterina de' Medici, an Florentine noble woman who married King Henry II of France, brought her favorite vegetable, spinach to the French court. She made it popular in France, and ever since then, dishes served with or on spinach are known as *alla Fiorentina* (or Florentine style, in her honor.)

Zucchine (Zucchini). Italians know to purchase their zucchini in the summer; these naturally grown zucchini are significantly more flavorful than others grown in hothouses out of season. This versatile vegetable can be used in sauces, salads, main courses, and almost any part of the Italian meal. Smaller zucchini have a more condensed flavor, and are much less bitter than larger, older, ones. Italians also love to fry the delicate flowers found on baby zucchini as a delicious treat.

FRUTTA, NOCI, E MISCELLANEA
Fruits, Nuts, and Miscellany

Acciughe, Alici. (Anchovies). There are many species of this small, salt-water fish. Although they are often eaten fresh from the sea in Italy, they are typically salted in brine, matured and then packed in oil in a jar or tin. Fresh anchovies have a much milder flavor. Anchovies are an essential ingredient in many Italian recipes, and are used in lieu of salt—they dissolve quickly and add a salty, rather than fishy flavor.

Brodo di Verdure (Vegetable Broth). Vegetable stock is a kitchen essential. It's as easy to make as it is to buy, which saves on waste. Rather than discarding the remains of the vegetables used in pasta recipes, cover them in water and boil them for an hour. Strain out solids, and store in the fridge for three days or freeze for up to three months. A simple recipe would include onion, carrot, celery, parsley, perhaps some salt and pepper, and any other vegetables around, like mushroom, fennel, tomato, etc.

Capperi (Capers). Capers are the flower bud from the thorny *Capparis spinosa* bush, edible once they have been cured. They grow wild on the southern coasts liking a dry, rocky spot; the farther south the better. Cultivation and harvesting is labor-intensive, having changed little from Roman times. The "caper berries" are harvested from plants which rarely reach a meter in height. As the buds are picked before blossoming, caper flowers are a rare sight. Capers are usually packed in oil or brine and therefore should generally be strained or rinsed before use.

Farina (Flour). In common usage, the term semolina is used for durum wheat flour, which is yellow in color and gives dry pasta its characteristic color. *Semolina* is derived from the Italian word *semola*, meaning "bran." *Durum* in Latin means «hard,» and the species is the hardest of all wheats. Its high protein content, as well as its strength, make durum an optimum choice for pasta secca (dry pasta). It is also the only legal one; Italian dry pasta is made, by law, exclusively from durum wheat. Although some homemade fresh pastas (pasta fresca), [such as orecchiette and cavatelli,] can use durum wheat, most pasta fresca (such as ravioli and tagliatelle,) utilize only soft wheat flours, like "00" (pastry flour) or "0" (all-purpose flour).

Limone (Lemon). Lemons are possibly the most widely used fruit in Italy, bringing flavor to other fruits as well as providing an acidic tang for fish, vegetable and pasta preparations; not to mention garnishing drinks of all types and adding zest to baked goods. Sicilian lemons have been renowned since the Middle Ages, when they provided steady income for the island. Today Sicily still provides Italy with 90 percent of its lemons. The lemons of the Amalfi coast in Campania also enjoy a wonderful reputation, where lemon groves abound in Sorrento and on Capri.

Mandorle (Almond). Originally from the Middle East, almonds are arguably the most-consumed nut in Italy. They flavor multitudes of desserts and drinks, as well as Arab-influenced savory dishes. The majority of Italy's almonds are grown in Puglia, but Emilia-Romana, especially in the Ferrara province and Sicily are also prominent producers.

Noci (Walnuts). Walnuts are an important part of many fillings and sauces, as well as a strong presence in sweets and desserts. The nut's slightly bitter taste is improved greatly by toasting. *Noci* are grown primarily in the Sorrento area of Campania as well as in Umbria. They make a great addition to many pasta sauces.

Olive e Olio d'Oliva (Olives and Olive Oil). With nearly 400 different olive varieties in Italy, most regions produce olive oil. The differences in regional climate and soil combined with this variation in fruit, produce both overt and subtle distinctions in taste, color and even texture of the resulting oil. These climatic differences also create their own balance of advantage and disadvantage.

Olio Extravergine (Extra Virgin Olive Oil). In order to be deemed Extra Virgin, an olive oil must meet many requirements and endure strict testing by the International Olive Council (IOC). Its acidity level must be under 1 percent, it must be extracted from the first pressing of the olives, and that extraction must be accomplished by mechanical, rather than chemical means, and under temperatures that will not damage the oil (less than 86°F, 30°C).

Olio Virgine (Virgin Olive Oil). Virgin oil must have an acidity level below 2 percent. Also one level down from Extra Virgin in terms of flavor, color and aroma, it is the oil one might cook with, but would never use as a condiment

Pepe (Pepper). *Piper nigrum* is a flowering vine in the family *Piperaceae*, which is usually dried and used as a spice. The fruit, known as a peppercorn, and the ground pepper derived from them, may be described simply as pepper, *pepe* or more precisely as *pepe nero* or black pepper (cooked and dried unripe fruit), *pepe verde* or green pepper (dried unripe fruit) and *pepe bianco* or white pepper (unripe fruit seeds). Dried ground pepper has been used since antiquity for both its flavor and medicinal uses.

Pinoli (Pine Nuts). Not really a nut per se, a pine nut is the seed within a pinecone that has been carefully dried, extracted from the cone and then dried again—a labor-intensive process that makes *pinoli* rather expensive. Delicious toasted and well-known as an ingredient in *Pesto Genovese*, *pinoli* are harvested specifically from the Mediterranean Stone Pine which has grown in Italy for as long as trees have stood there.

Pistacchio (Pistachio). Although it may grow in other parts of southern Italy, the pistachio is a Sicilian specialty. The details of its original arrival are somewhat murky, but it was during the period of Arab domination that pistachio cultivation began in earnest. The *Pistachio Verde di Bronte* DOP gets its rich flavor from being grown directly on the lava of Mount Etna.

Sale (Salt). Good Italian chefs use salt. But never too much salt. Of course, this is easier when your ingredients are fresh. Because table salt may contain additives like iodine, natural sea salt or other natural salts are always preferred. Kosher salt, with large irregularly shaped flakes, is good for meats. Salt has been used to preserve food for millennia. As a matter of fact, the word "salary" comes from the Latin term "salarium" which was the name for a soldier's pay in the army of ancient Rome. Their pay included a ration of salt, which was a spice of high value and also used for barter. Hence the expression, "worth your salt."

Sarde (Sardines). Deboning sardines is no easy task, so you should admire the Sicilian women on the coast near Agrigento who do it every day in the sardine factory. They have a special word for what they do: Scamozzare (for taking off the head and removing the spine of sardines). I assure you that they will do this faster and more accurately than you ever will. If you can't locate Mediterranean sardines, you will need to use the Atlantic variety, which may have larger bones. If so, you will either need to spend more time deboning them, or do the best you can and then put them into a food processor to ensure the bones are sufficiently miniscule. Ideally, you will use the Mediterranean *sarde*, debone them, and then cut them into bite-sized pieces.

PASTA BASICS

← Timpano Pantheon. See inside and recipe on page 128.

A Brief History of Pasta

Did the Italians invent pasta? Probably not. Did Marco Polo bring pasta back to Italy from China? Absolutely not. What is certain is that the Italians have elevated the preparation of pasta to an art form, unsurpassed anywhere in the world. Pasta is the most popular *primo* (first course) choice in Italy, and is often the main course. Although it may compete with *zuppa* (soup) and *polenta* in some central and northern regions of Italy, within the everyday meal, pasta is a point of national gustatory pride and arguably Italy's emblematic dish. As the Italian statesman Garibaldi once said, "It is maccheroni, I swear to you, that will unify Italy."

Fresh pasta's (*pasta fresca*) journey probably began two millennia ago, with the Roman *laganum*, a crude precursor to lasagna. Dried pasta *(pasta secca)* began with the Arabs, in Sicily after the Arab invasion/occupation in the 9th century AD. Although it is not certain when it began exactly, pasta production was definitely established on a significant scale in Palermo by the 10th century. (Their term *maccheroni* (macaroni*)* comes from the Italian, "macchinare," for the hard word needed to make it by hand; it continues to be the umbrella term for pasta.) Centuries later, pasta had spread around Italy. Genovese sailors, Christopher Columbus included, enjoyed "little worms" or *vermicelli* on their long voyages. The development of a mechanized press and a more efficient kneading system in the 17th century lowered production costs, making it more affordable. By 1785, Naples was the hub of pasta production boasting 280 different pasta shops.

Meanwhile, since the Middle Ages in the Po Valley and other inland areas, *pasta fresca* was being made daily in private homes. It contained eggs in the north, a plentiful commodity there, as well as soft flour, or farina. Southern variations were made with semolina and without eggs. Filled pasta or *pasta ripiena* had its place as a luxury dish. It was because of the slippery quality of pasta that in the 14th century Italians began using forks to eat, well before their European neighbors.

With the unification of Italy, pasta—*secca and fresca*—would eventually become a food category with almost infinite regional varieties, rather than a vast number of unrelated dishes. Perhaps Garibaldi had a point. Since the mid-twentieth century, pasta has enjoyed preferred *primo* status in Italy, as well as becoming a global favorite and one of Italy's most popular exports.

Methods of preparation

Even with more than 500 long, short, tubular, filled and colored varieties, pasta today still divides into two types, *secca* and *fresca*, each having its own distinct ingredients and methods of preparation.

Pasta Secca (Dry Pasta)

The most important element of dry pasta is the wheat, which must be hard grain. Once pasta production began in earnest, Sicily expanded its wheat output for the pasta, but there was also a strong tradition of wheat importation in Italy. To make the dough, the whole grain of wheat was combined with water where it would break down. Genoa and Naples, Italy's two leading pasta producers had slightly different mechanical methods for doing this—Genoa used a circular mill and Naples a plunging mill operated by foot pumps. Extrusion through bronze dies or discs left a surface roughness that, along with the chemical reaction that occurred in cooking, allowed the pasta to grab and absorb as much sauce as possible. Last, the sunshine and breezes of these cities provided the perfect climate for the pasta, hanging on wooden posts, to dry, at just the right speed to maintain taste and texture.

The 1930 invention of the pasta press turned pasta making into one continuous process and sped up production considerably. Drying units that simulated the optimal drying climate, invented after WWII, made pasta making not nearly as dependent on location. With the countrywide spread of dried pasta came the law—number 580, enacted in 1976—regulating the production of flours and breads, as well as pastas.

With its long, rich history, pasta production has come a long way. The use of stainless steel, aluminum or plastic dies and quick-drying is a lamentable by-product of insatiable demand. The "Purity Law" states that the wheat used still must be durum semolina to make Italian pasta. And with the popular promotion of traditional methods in other foods as well as pasta, many companies are proudly describing their use of bronze dies and slow drying practices.

Pasta Fresca (Fresh Pasta)

If you have seen a cooking show in the past ten years or so, you must have seen a mound or *fontana* (fountain) of flour with a well in the middle, waiting for the addition of water and/or eggs, to be transformed into fresh pasta. Pasta has been made this way, rolled out by hand, since the Middle Ages. The pasta machine that will make the *sfoglia* (sheet of dough) finer and finer with each pass is an advance to some, but causes an unacceptable change in finished texture—too smooth—to others.

With the exception of full-scale commercial production, where the finished product will keep for a suspicious two weeks instead of a day, very little has changed in the world of fresh pasta. However, even though it can always be made at home, busy working families now frequently buy their handmade fresh pasta locally. Although it is everywhere in Italy, Emilia-Romagna's *pasta fresca* is the most renowned. And here, as well as in other northern regions, the sauces are likely to contain butter or cream and sometimes both, rather than olive oil and tomato.

Pasta Ripiena (Filled Pasta)

A subset, if you will, of *pasta fresca* is *pasta ripiena* or filled pasta. It has evolved, as the ravioli of the Middle Ages were meat dumplings with no dough encasing them. The idea of *pasta ripiena* as we know it could have been inspired by either a desire to use banquet leftovers or show off the most prized and expensive meats and cheeses in the house. Either way, filled pasta is complex already and so usually served simply, in broth or with butter, sometimes with a very simple sauce. Because of the multiple thicknesses of its dough, it also offers a nice treat in differing textures. And because of its intrinsic fragility, it is important to prepare pasta *ripiena* in simmering rather than boiling water to avoid explosions and losses of filling during cooking.

Forme di Pasta (Pasta Shapes)

Each of the Italian regions has a number of types of pasta, all fresh and hand made. And the commercial pasta industry is continually producing more and more types of dry pasta named after some regional shape.

With so many, the table at the back of the book will help you to keep your pastas straight, but they can be generally classified, with their most common examples, as follows:

- **Pasta Lunga (Long Strands):** capellini, spaghetti, linguine
- **Fettuce (Ribbons):** fettucine, pappardelle, tagliatelle
- **Tubi Lunghi (Long Tubes):** bucatini, perciatelli
- **Tubi Corti (Short tubes):** ziti, rigatoni, penne
- **Pasta Piccola (Small Shapes):** acini di pepe, pastina, orzo, stelle
- **Forme Uniche (Unique Shapes):** orecchiette, fusilli, farfalle
- **Ripieni (Filled):** tortellini, ravioli, manicotti, cannelloni

Pasta Artigianale (Artisanal Pasta)

Even if you cannot make it at home, some Italians eat only *pasta artigianale*, or artisanal pasta, made in small factories, the old-fashioned way, with a slow drying process. This pasta often has a rougher surface, which is better for holding sauce. Some say that it retains a higher nutritional value.

Cooking Pasta

Requirements:

1. A large, good quality pot with a heavy bottom (for constant heat).
2. A container to measure water: the ideal ratio is 6 quarts to 1 pound of pasta.
3. 1 pound (one package) serves 4 to 6 persons. (The Italians generally calculate 100 grams per person, about $\frac{1}{5}$ of a pound.)
4. Always cook the pasta in copiously salted water.
5. Add the pasta when the water is boiling. Cook until *al dente* (firm to the tooth—about 2 minutes less than the package directions), stirring and tasting often.
6. Immediately remove the pasta from the heat, then drain, leaving it slightly damp.
7. At this point, add to the skillet containing the sauce, or to a serving bowl and then add the sauce (according to the recipe).
8. Serve Immediately.

THE DO'S and DON'TS of PASTA

- Do not add oil to the water. *But do add salt.*
- Do not overcook it. *It should be al dente, or firm and chewy.*
- Do not throw it at the wall. *Bite into it to see if it is done.*
- Drain it, *but do not rinse it.*
- Dress it with sauce, *but do not drown it.*
- When appropriate, sprinkle cheese on it, *but do not smother it.*
- Twirl it with a fork if it's a long variety, *but not with a spoon.*
- And please, *no knives.*

BASIC PASTA RECIPE

Making homemade pasta can be both fun and rewarding. It is not difficult to do, and with some practice it is easy to learn to make all sorts of shapes, sizes, and colors of pasta. That said, it can also be time consuming. Luckily for all of us, there is now a wide range of quality dry pastas available at most grocery stores, and many now carry fresh and filled pastas. If you want to make homemade pasta, the following recipe is easy to follow. You can always add spinach, beet juice, tomato paste, squid ink, or even cocoa, to create pasta in one of the many different colors and flavors you often find in stores and restaurants. Regardless of whether you make it from scratch, remember that the process should be fun, and that the main point of *Sunday Pasta* is to enjoy time with family or friends!

Ingredients

2 ½ cups 00 flour (or 0 flour, which is all-purpose flour)

Pinch of salt

3 eggs, beaten

Salt to taste

Directions

Make a mound with the flour on a clean work surface. Make a well in the middle of the flour and add a pinch of salt and the beaten eggs. Use a fork to carefully incorporate the eggs with the flour. When thoroughly combined, use your hands to knead the dough for 10 minutes until smooth. (Of course, you can use a kitchen mixer with a knead attachment to accomplish this task). Tightly enclose the dough in plastic wrap and set aside for 20 minutes. (The quantity of flour to egg may vary depending on egg size, flour type, and other factors.)

Cut the dough into 4–6 pieces of equal size. Use only one piece at a time (leaving the remaining dough wrapped in plastic). If you are doing this the-old fashioned way, use a rolling pin to roll it out on a dry, floured surface—fold it back and roll again. Repeat this process until a thin sheet of pasta is achieved. Alternatively, pass it through a pasta machine until thin, or until it goes through the second thinnest setting at least twice. At this point, you can cut the pasta to the desired length, shape, and width. After cutting the pasta, you can cook it immediately or refrigerate it for up to two days or freeze up to two weeks. (Before storing, let it dry for a couple of minutes, dust with flour, let dry for another 30 minutes, then fold into the familiar nest shape, and wrap in plastic.)

SALSA DI POMODORO
Tomato Sauce

There are hundreds of pasta recipes that involve tomatoes, with at least as many names for their sauces. With so many regions and dialects in Italy and a global emigration, it should be no surprise that the many names for the sauces have been incorrectly altered or utilized. Let's start at the beginning. In the beginning… there was *sugo di pomodoro*…

In Italian, a basic tomato sauce is called a *sugo di pomodoro* or a *salsa al pomodoro*. The term "marinara sauce" is an inaccurate American term for this simple sauce, as a marinara sauce in Italy would probably include some sort of seafood. Nor is it correct to refer to a simple tomato sauce as a "gravy," which would translate closer to a *ragu*, generally from Naples, in which some sort of meat is slowly cooked in the tomato sauce.

For the basic sauce, start with the core ingredients: tomato, onion, olive oil, salt, and pepper. From here, additional ingredients may be added. Basil is typically the first addition, and then some might add carrots, celery, parsley, oregano, etc. and then of course, sausage, ground veal, or pork. It all depends on your tastes and traditions. Just note that the more you add, the less likely it is a simple tomato sauce.

Tomato sauce can be made with fresh or canned tomatoes, can be smooth or chunky and can be cooked for a long or short period of time. It all depends on the mood, the season, the type of pasta served with it, and the time available.

The following recipe is in this section of the book because it is the basis of so many other pasta recipes. Simple and delicious, it captures the essence of Sunday Pasta!

PENNE AL SUGO DI POMODORO
Penne with Tomato Sauce

The secret to happiness (and perhaps sanity) is found somewhere between "Ball of Confusion" by The Temptations and my grandmother Virginia's tomato sauce recipe. You should listen to the 1970 song while reading the lyrics for maximum effect. In that poetry, you'll see that the world is very much the same ball of confusion that it was more than 40 years ago, as it probably was 400 years ago and probably will be 400 years from now. To expect otherwise is pointless. On the other hand, my Nanni's tomato sauce is constant: simple, delicious, and easy to share. No confusion here, just peace, love, and understanding. So, savor the moment… and the sauce!

Serves 4–6

- 1 onion, finely chopped
- ½ cup olive oil
- 1 28-ounce can peeled plum tomatoes, puréed
- 1 teaspoon salt
- ½ teaspoon freshly ground black pepper
- 4–6 basil leaves, coarsely chopped
- 1 tablespoon sugar—optional
- 1 pound penne—or any pasta
- Grated Parmigiano for serving

Bring a large pot of salted water to a boil.

In a large skillet over medium heat, sauté the onion in the olive oil until golden. Add the tomatoes, salt and pepper. Add the basil, and a little sugar as desired. Lower the heat and simmer until reduced, 20–30 minutes.

Cook the pasta until *al dente* (about 2 minutes less than package directions). Drain, add to the sauce, and mix together over medium heat.

Serve immediately with grated Parmigiano.

Note: The above measures are a guide, but add or subtract to taste. Nanni used a food mill to purée canned tomatoes and remove the seeds—which are said to have a slightly bitter taste. I rarely use one and instead rely on a speedy blender. Sugar is a controversial addition. My grandmother preferred a slightly sweet sauce and so added it, citing the fact that canned tomatoes are more bitter than fresh ones. I rarely add it. She would not add it to sauces with meat, such as a ragú.

VINO

Bianco: Vermentino
Rosso: Sangiovese Blends

This pasta sings with the brightness of tomato-driven acidity and sweetness in a dish of moderate weight. For a white wine, Vermentino straddles the line between medium and full-bodied, thus supporting the weight of the pasta itself. For a red, choose Sangiovese-dominant blends from Tuscany, which smell of tomato leaf and tingle with acidity that aligns with this tomato sauce.

SPRING RECIPES

RAVIOLI DI SPINACI AL BURRO E SALVIA

Spinach Ravioli with Butter and Sage

A penny for your thoughts … It's time for a little pillow talk, Italian style. And since any and all Italian conversations lead back to food, let's talk about the delicious, soft pillows that are ravioli.

A ravioli by any other name would taste as sweet … Although the term ravioli is used broadly for filled pasta, the many names, shapes, and sizes change regionally. From *agnolotti* to *triangoli*, from *anolini* to *pansotti* to *tortellini*, it all depends on the locale, and then the filling and the shape … and of course, local pride and custom.

The photograph shows *ravioli a mezzaluna* (half-moons) filled with ricotta and spinach. They're served in a simple butter sage sauce. To be sure, you can buy decent ravioli at a good Italian market. Or you can spend a few hours making spectacular ravioli at home. I like to recruit my family and make a party out of it.

Serves 4–6

See Basic Pasta Recipe.
  See inside and recipe on page 28

Filling

2 cups whole milk ricotta cheese

2 eggs

2 tablespoons grated Parmigiano, plus more to serve

2 cups spinach, cooked, squeezed dry, and chopped

Freshly ground black pepper to taste

2 egg yolks moistened with a bit of water

Sauce

8 fresh sage leaves

½ cup butter

In a large bowl, use a wooden spoon to beat the ricotta for a minute or until smooth. Beat in the eggs and add the cheese. Mix in the spinach, salt and pepper to taste.

Cut the dough into 4–6 pieces of equal size. Use only one piece at a time (leaving the remaining dough wrapped in plastic). If you are doing this the-old fashioned way, use a rolling pin to roll it out on a dry, floured surface—fold it back and roll again. Repeat this process until a thin sheet of pasta is achieved. Alternatively, pass it through a pasta machine until thin, or until it goes through the second thinnest setting at least twice. Use a 2-inch cookie or biscuit cutter, or juice glass to cut the pasta into rounds.

Add the spinach-ricotta filling to the middle of the round. Use your finger to dab the edges with egg yolk. Fold in half and use your fingers or a fork to press down and seal. Repeat this process until all of the dough and filling are used.

Bring a large pot of salted water to a gentle boil.

Heat the butter in a skillet, add the sage and cook until the butter browns.

Add the ravioli to the boiling water and cook for 3–4 minutes after they float to the top. Use a wire mesh strainer or slotted spoon to remove them from the pot and add to a warm serving dish. Pour the butter and sage sauce over the ravioli.

Serve immediately with grated Parmigiano.

VINO

Bianco: Sauvignon Blanc and Blends
Rosso: Barbera

Sage is a delicately fragrant herb, so lightly herbal wines make an enticing match. The dish's dairy components need a wine with at least medium body, perhaps some mid-palate creaminess. For whites, look to Friuli for Sauvignon Blanc, with its cut grass and green bean notes, especially those that are barrel-fermented. Juicy Piedmont reds are a strong match here, especially Piedmont's "everyday" Barbera grape. Look for a mid-weight Barbera d'Alba.

RIGATONI ALLA GRICIA

Rigatoni with Pancetta and Onion

I'm as mad as hell, and I'm not going to take this anymore. I'm fighting mad. Fit to be tied. Go ahead, make my day. Let's take this outside.

I was recently in a NYC Italian restaurant and asked the waiter for a menu suggestion. His response, "Well, do you eat pasta?" Noticing my look of disgust, he defensively continued, "Well, we *are* in New York City you know." Yes, I know, New York City (like Los Angeles) where AK-47's are considered safer than carbohydrates.

I'm tired of all of the pasta bashing. Twenty years ago, Americans ate only carbohydrates and the country was thinner than it is now. The average Italian consumes three times as much pasta as the average American. Other than what is being caused by imported processed foods and sodas, there is no obesity epidemic in Italy. So listen to me all of you carbophobic pasta bullies, you leave my friend pasta alone. A bowl of pasta will not make you fat; a mountain of pasta may. Eat the pasta, and make it an Italian-sized portion. It will make you happy. Endorphins and serotonin will set you free. And then take a walk, with a smile on your face. Basta. Enough already. Mangia.

Serves 4–6

- 6 ounces pancetta or guanciale
- ½ cup olive oil
- 3 medium onions, thinly sliced
- ½ cup grated Pecorino Romano cheese
- 1 pound rigatoni or other tubular pasta
- Freshly ground black pepper to taste

Cut the pancetta into ½ inch strips or small cubes.

In a large skillet over medium heat, sauté the pancetta in the olive oil. After a minute or two, add the onion. Cook over low heat until the onion is golden.

Bring a large pot of salted water to a boil.

Cook the pasta until *al dente* (about 2 minutes less than package directions). Drain, and retain about one cup of cooking liquid. Add pasta to the pancetta and onion, mix well, and cook over medium heat for minute. Add some of the retained water if it looks dry.

Place the pasta in a serving bowl, add the Pecorino and a generous amount of black pepper. Mix well.

Serve immediately.

Note: In Rome, guanciale is often used, but I prefer the meatier pancetta. See page 16.

VINO

Bianco: Trebbiano d'Abruzzo
Rosso: Montepulciano d'Abruzzo

Pancetta makes this moderately rich pasta dish very savory, so the best pairings should either be equally savory or sharply in contrast with a chunky fruitiness. The white Trebbiano grape is neutral, showing only the faintest fruit. Reds from the Montepulciano d'Abruzzo grape could not be more different, but they work just as well, offering a touch more acidity and a light layer of tannin to keep the palate fresh.

FUSILLI CON TONNO E POMODORINI

Fusilli with Tuna and Cherry Tomatoes

I don't want to come off sounding like one of those nut jobs ranting about how processed food and fast food are slowly killing America. Well, actually, I do. Call me a communist or a socialist or whatever, but I see no reason why only rich people should be able to afford to eat healthy food, while everyone else has to pick their poison. Now, don't get me wrong, I like penthouses and yachts as much as the next guy, but not everyone can afford to shop at Whole Foods, affectionately referred to as "Whole Paycheck."

We won't fix this problem overnight, but we can start by changing the way we think about food. To get my kids headed in the right direction, I've come up with the following nicknames for our daily drive-bys: McDonald's is now "CrapDonald's," KFC is "Kentucky Fat Chicken," Burger King is "Burger Kringe," and Taco Bell is "Taco Hell."

The following recipe feeds a family of four for about $15 total. It takes less than 30 minutes to prepare, and is chock full of protein, carbohydrates, some healthy fats, and lots of vitamins and minerals. It's fast food that can make a nation strong!

Serves 4–6

1 onion, finely chopped

½ cup olive oil

1 pound cherry tomatoes, rinsed, stems removed, cut in half

10 ounces canned tuna, packed in olive oil, drained, flaked

¼ cup chopped flat-leaf parsley

Salt to taste

Freshly ground black pepper to taste

1 pound fusilli

In a large skillet, over medium heat, sauté the onion in the olive oil until golden. Add the tomatoes and cook for about 10 minutes, or until some of the tomato juices evaporate. Mix in the tuna, half of the parsley and salt and pepper to taste. Cook for five more minutes.

Bring a large pot of salted water to boil.

Cook the pasta until *al dente* (about 2 minutes less than package directions). Drain and add it to the tuna. Cook together for one minute.

Serve immediately, with the remaining parsley.

VINO

Bianco: Vermentino

Rosato: Tuscan Blends

Tuna is a dense fish, whether canned or fresh, and can pair well with a light red. However, the sweet-tart pop of cherry tomatoes works better with white and rosé wines. Vermentino's racy acidity will match the tomatoes' tanginess, and its aromatic verve will equal the parsley's pop. For some extra body, try just about any rosato blend from Tuscany, with red fruit flavors to link with the tomato sauce.

CAPRICCI PRIMAVERA (ALL'ORTOLANO)
Capricci with Garden Vegetables

Aaah, *La Primavera*. Springtime. Fresh air, fresh flowers, and a fresh desire to drop ten pounds. What better way to kick-off the spring season than with a bowl of pasta and fresh vegetables? Pasta Primavera became popular in America in the 1970's. In Italy, it is more commonly called *Pasta all'Ortolano* (gardener's pasta). The beauty of the dish is that you can use whatever vegetables you like or have on hand. Some people (not Italians) will add cream, but I think it destroys the light and fresh purpose of the dish.

I can't help but wonder what actually led someone to add cream to this dish in the first place. What were they thinking?! What Philistine did this? "RAPE OF CUISINE!" as Primo yells in *Big Night*.

But I certainly don't want to cloud the delights of springtime with such negative thoughts. So, just grow or go out and buy the, freshest, most beautiful vegetables you can find, chop them up, sauté them in olive oil, and pour them over your favorite pasta. Do something good for yourself. After all, summer is just around the corner.

Serves 4

About ½ cup of each of the following—no need to be precise. Add or subtract to taste.

1 small onion, finely chopped

1 carrot, peeled, finely chopped

1 stalk celery, finely chopped

½ cup olive oil

6 asparagus stems woody ends removed, cut into ½ inch pieces red pepper, coarsely chopped

1 red pepper, coarsely chopped

1 zucchini, coarsely chopped

¼ cup finely chopped flat-leaf parsley

Salt to taste

Freshly ground black pepper to taste

1 pound capricci (or penne, farfalle)

Grated Parmigiano

In a large skillet over medium heat, sauté the onion, carrot, and celery in the olive oil until the onion is translucent. Add the asparagus and cook for 5 minutes. Add the red pepper and cook for 5 more minutes.

Bring a large pot of salted water to a boil.

Add the zucchini, and about a teaspoon of salt and pepper, and cook for an additional 5–10 minutes, or until the vegetables are thoroughly cooked, but not too soft.

Cook the pasta until *al dente* (about 2 minutes less than package directions), drain, and retain a cup of the cooking water. Add the pasta to the vegetables and mix together. Add a bit of the cooking water if it seems too dry.

Toss in the parsley and serve, with grated Parmigiano.

VINO

Bianco: Pinot Grigio
Rosato: Pinot Grigio

Pinot Grigio is a slightly odd grape. Its pulp is actually pink, and its style changes dramatically as it ripens. When picked early at lower ripeness, it produces a pale, lightly fruit-driven wine with loads of minerality, earthy undertones and lower alcohol. At higher ripeness levels, the fruit flavors border tropical, the wine boasts more body, and the color can be copper. Regardless of which style you choose, Pinot Grigio's flavors will meld well with the tender spring vegetables.

TAGLIATELLE ALLA BOLOGNESE
Tagliatelle with Meat Sauce

"Luuuucy, I'm hoooome." To me, Ricky Ricardo was e*thnic*; I was just a guy from New Jersey. (Ok, so maybe I sported a gold cross, drove a Firebird, had big hair, and my father's name was Mario, but hey, I wore Polo shirts!) So, you can imagine the shock I experienced in college when my very blonde date ordered *Spaghetti Bolognese* and then picked up her knife and started to cut. Cringing inside, but charming as ever, I smiled and said, "Ooooh, please don't cut your pasta." She flatly replied, "Don't get ethnic with me, Ed." What? Who? Me? Ethnic?

Many years later, needless to say, I am happily ethnic and still courageously educating about pasta etiquette. So forgive me for getting ethnic with you, but please leave the knife and spoon on the table and learn to twirl with a fork. (And yes, if you're among friends, you can use a little piece of bread for assistance.)

The recipe below is based on that of Chef Dean Caselnova in Brooklyn, who learned at Papa Re Trattoria and Trattoria dalla Gigina in Bologna. It's the real deal, from Bologna via Brooklyn. Mamma Mia! Now that's Italian! (Big pinch to right cheek.)

Serves 4–6

1 onion, coarsely chopped
1 celery stalk, finely chopped
1 carrot, peeled, finely chopped
1 bay leaf
¼ cup olive oil
¾ pound ground beef—20 percent fat is best
¼ pound ground pork
3 slices prosciutto, finely chopped
1 6-ounce can tomato paste
½ cup dry white wine
1-35 ounce can plum tomatoes, puréed
1 pound tagliatelle (or spaghetti)

In a large, heavy-bottom pot over medium heat sauté the onion, celery, carrot and bay leaf in the olive oil until onion is translucent. Add ground beef, pork, and prosciutto to the sautéed vegetables and use a wooden spoon to break up the meat. When meat is nearly cooked, add tomato paste and stir to fully incorporate. Add white wine and simmer until the wine evaporates. Add the crushed tomatoes and ½ can (from the tomatoes) of water.

Bring the sauce to a boil and then reduce to a simmer. Cook, uncovered for approximately 2 hours. Add salt to taste.

Bring a large pot of salted water to a boil.

Cook the tagliatelle until *al dente* (about 2 minutes less than package directions). Drain, add to the Bolognese sauce and stir to combine. Serve immediately.

VINO
Rosso: Sangiovese di Romagna

With a base of tomato sauce, beef, and pork, this classic pasta begs for a red wine. As it hails from Bologna, it seems most appropriate to pair it with a wine crafted in the region, such as a Sangiovese di Romagna. Similar to Sangiovese from Tuscany, the Romagna version has mouth-watering acidity and cherry flavors as well as its own unique, fresh herb, aromatic lift.

CALAMARATA CON GAMBERI E ASPARAGI

Calamarata with Shrimp and Asparagus

I always knew that Forrest Gump wasn't the savant people made him out to be. Sure he made a fortune, walked a lot, and was wildly popular, but could he cook? I think not. He showed his hand during his litany of ways to prepare shrimp: "You can barbecue it, boil it, broil it, bake it … lemon shrimp, coconut shrimp, [blah, blah, blah] shrimp … That's, that's about it." Wrong, Forrest! His rookie error? He forgot one of the most obvious and delicious ways ever to cook shrimp: with pasta! Just imagine if he had said, in perfect Italian, "*Jenny, lo so che stai morendo, ti ho fatto un piatto gustoso di pasta con gamberi e asparagi per farti godere il tuo ultimo pasto.*" (Translation: "Jenny, I know you're dying, so I've made you a tasty bowl of *farfalle con gamberi e asparagi* for you to enjoy as your last meal.") Now that would have been both impressive and dramatic. But no, like the dish itself, Forrest was just simple, healthy … and yes, crowd pleasing.

Serves 4–6

- 1 bunch asparagus, tough woody ends removed, cut into ½-inch pieces
- 1 onion, finely chopped
- 2 tablespoons olive oil
- 1 pound shrimp, peeled and deveined, cut into 1-inch pieces
- 1 cup white wine
- Salt and pepper
- 1 pound calamarata (penne or other short pasta)

Bring a large pot of water to boil. Add the salt to the water after you cook the asparagus.

Add the asparagus to the boiling water and cook for 3 minutes. Remove with a wire mesh strainer or slotted spoon and reserve.

In a large skillet, over medium heat, sauté the onion in the olive oil until golden. Add the asparagus and sauté together for a few minutes and then add the shrimp. After another minute (longer if the shrimp is not pre-cooked), add the white wine. Add some salt and cook the combined ingredients over medium heat for two additional minutes.

Cook the pasta until *al dente* (about 2 minutes less than package directions), and retain 1 cup of the cooking water. Drain the pasta and add it to the shrimp and asparagus. Cook together for 1 minute, adding the retained cooking water as needed to make sure the pasta is moist and well coated. Serve immediately.

VINO

Bianco: Gavi di Gavi

Rosso: Val d'Aosta Blends

Asparagus can be difficult to pair with wine because of its grassy flavors. Grape varieties with herbal notes and wines from cool climates – which often show herbal edges – make the best pairings. Most of Val d'Aosta's light-bodied and pale-colored reds are blends. They tend to show a just-ripe character that hints at green, just right for the asparagus and also have very light tannin that does not clash with the shrimp.

PENNE AL PISTACCHIO

Penne with Pistachios

Let us ponder the pistachio: On the menu since the Upper Paleolithic, one of two nuts mentioned in the Bible, often dyed red like Twizzlers for the benefit of our children. So much work, so little food, so painful for our fingers. So why, you ask, does the pistachio endure? Why? I don't want to oversimplify matters, but my hunch is that humans have been eating pistachios for over 10,000 years mainly because they taste good … even on pasta.

The most delicious pistachio in Italy (and therefore in the world) is the *Pistacchio di Bronte DOP*, which is government protected. Let's face it, as an immigrant from Persia (Iran) via Syria to Sicily over 2000 years ago, this pistachio has got to be one tough nut. I doubt you'll find real *Pistacchio di Bronte* locally, so you'll just have to live with the nuts from California …

Serves 4–6

- 1 cup pistachio nuts unsalted and shelled
- 1 onion, finely chopped
- 2 tablespoons olive oil
- 2 tablespoons butter
- 1 slice of prosciutto or pancetta, chopped (optional)
- 1 cup white wine (optional)
- 1 cup heavy cream
- Salt to taste
- Freshly ground pepper to taste
- 1 pound penne

Finely chop the pistachios in a food processor or coffee grinder. Set aside one quarter of the ground nuts for garnish.

In a large skillet, over medium heat, sauté the onion in the olive oil and butter until it's golden. Add the prosciutto and cook one minute; it should not become crispy. Add the pistachios and toss until well-coated with the other ingredients. Add the white wine and cook for 3 minutes. Add the cream, salt and pepper. Cook until the cream is slightly reduced, 4 or 5 minutes.

Bring a large pot of salted water to a boil. Cook the pasta until *al dente* (about 2 minutes less than package directions), drain, and retain 1 cup of the cooking water. Add the pasta to the skillet with the pistachio mixture and stir together for about a minute. Add some of the retained cooking water if it seems too dry.

Serve, garnished with the remaining chopped pistachios.

Note: If you cannot find unsalted pistachios at the market, rinse the shelled pistachios in cold water to remove the salt and loose skins and pat dry.

VINO

Bianco: Friulano Blends

Rosso: Valpolicella or Corvina Blends

This pasta makes for a complex pairing between the lighter, green nuttiness of the pistachios and the heavier aspects of pancetta and heavy cream. It needs a wine with similar heft along with either contrasting, soaring acidity, or complementary, mouth-coating texture. Friuli crafts complex white blends with both heft and acidic tension. Reds with a pronounced red fruit character, like Valpolicella, based on Covina, give a nice fruitiness to contrast with the richness of this dish.

PAGLIA E FIENO

Tagliatelle with Prosciutto, Cream, and Peas

I currently live out in the country, where many of my neighbors are horses. This, as opposed to life in New York City, where many of my neighbors were merely asses. And while I certainly do miss the city's rich cultural offerings, I am beginning to embrace bucolic living.

One major disadvantage, though, is that while asses can be entertaining dinner guests, horses are just no good for witty conversation. Luckily, where horses go, go horsey people. And even though they may dress like it's 1950, I share with them a common fondness for pinot noir, proving once again what everyone in Umbria already knows: A beautiful view, a bowl of pasta, and a few guffaws is all you really need to be happy.

Surprisingly, horses have also taught me a couple things about Italian cuisine. For example, "*paglia e fieno*" translates into "straw and hay." Hay is green (and is eaten by the horse) and straw is yellow (and is used for the horse to sleep on). This rustic favorite from Emilia-Romagna is generally made with the combination of yellow and green tagliatelle. Some people add peas or mushrooms (or both), plus prosciutto and cream. You'll love it regardless of whether your neighbors are horses or asses.

Serves 4–6

- 1 small onion, finely chopped
- 4 ounces butter
- 6 ounces prosciutto, thickly sliced, and cut into strips
- 1 cup heavy cream
- 12 ounces peas, thawed if frozen
- Salt to taste
- Freshly ground pepper to taste
- ½ cup grated Parmigiano
- ½ pound green and ½ pound yellow tagliatelle

Bring a large pot of salted water to a boil.

In a large skillet over medium heat sauté the onion in the butter until it's golden brown. Add the prosciutto and cook for 1 minute. Add the cream, peas, salt and pepper and cook until slightly reduced, about 5 minutes.

Cook the pasta until *al dente* (about 2 minutes less than package directions), drain, and add to cream mixture. Remove from heat and mix in the Parmigiano.

Serve immediately.

VINO

Bianco: Albana di Romagna
Rosso: Lambrusco (Dry)

Heavy cream, butter and prosciutto require wines with equal weight but good acidic lift. Albana di Romagna is a medium-plus to full-bodied wine. When oak-aged, it exhibits notes of cream and brioche that match this pasta. Alternatively, Emilia-Romagna's signature fizz, dry Lambrusco, provides mouth-cleansing relief between its bubbles and delicate tannins.

SPAGHETTI AI CARCIOFI
Spaghetti with Artichokes

There are a few tidbits from 20th century television that have left an indelible mark on my psyche. First, I still quack and refer to people as my "fine feathered friends" in honor of Batman's nemesis, The Penguin. Second, I cannot drive through Beverly Hills without singing "and up from the ground came abubblin' crude" in honor of the Hillbillies (noting that the Clampetts are still there, alive and well in spirit). And third, my favorite, I cannot look at an artichoke without thinking "Mighta choked Artie, but it ain't gonna choke Stymie," in honor of The Little Rascals. (Now, please don't tell me that American culture is not in decline…)

If an Artie ever does choke me, it will be because I loved them too much. Fried, sautéed, baked, boiled, braised, roasted, steamed, stuffed, moussed, terrined, in soup, in stew, with lamb, with beef, with fish, shaved with Parmigiano … even fermented into the nasty and delicious Cynar. Big, small, baby, leaves, heart, and stem, I love artichokes. And when married with pasta? Try it, and you are certain to "Live Long and Prosper."

Serves 4–6

1 lemon

4 large or 8 small artichokes

2–3 cloves garlic, finely chopped

½ cup olive oil

2 cups chicken or vegetable broth—or water and white wine

1 tablespoon finely chopped flat-leaf parsley

Salt to taste

Freshly ground black pepper to taste

1 pound spaghetti, with this dish long pasta and short pasta work equally well

Grated Parmigiano

Fill a bowl with cold water and the juice of one lemon. Remove the tough outer leaves from the artichokes. Cut off the stem. Place the artichoke on its side and cut off the tops of the remaining leaves. Cut the artichokes in half, lengthwise, use a sharp knife to remove the fuzzy choke, and cut each side into thin pieces—depending on size, this will result in 4–6 slices per half. Place the pieces in the lemon water to prevent discoloration.

In a large saucepan over medium heat, sauté the garlic in the olive oil until it begins to turn gold and add the broth. Add the artichokes and simmer for 20 minutes.

Bring a large pot of salted water to a boil.

Add the parsley, salt and pepper to taste to the artichokes.

Cook the pasta until almost *al dente* (about 2 minutes less than package directions), drain, and add it to the artichokes. Heat together for a minute.

Serve immediately with grated Parmigiano.

Note: in lieu of broth, you can use water, or 1 cup of white wine, or a combination of liquids.

VINO
Bianco: Aspirinio, Pigato, or Gavi di Gavi

Artichoke complicates wine pairings. The chemical at work is cynarin, which lends artichokes their bitterness. Italian reds' pronounced tannins are accentuated further by this bitterness, so stick with whites. Look to match the light, fresh, and acidic characteristics of artichokes with Aspirinio and Pigato. These lesser-known grape varieties pair well with artichokes thanks to their nuttiness and strong citrus tones. Gavi di Gavi also works if these other options are not available.

BUCATINI CON LE SARDE
Bucatini with Sardines

Oy, the things I do for you. I endured Magnifica Class on Alitalia and then traversed an arid, rugged terrain, covered with ancient ruins. I baked in the hot Sicilian sun and burned the bottoms of my feet on the shores of the Ionian Sea. I ate to the point of discomfort over and over again, while tasting a variety of delicious but unforgiving wines. (I can't even begin to discuss the pain inflicted on me by my friend, Signor Grappa.) I barely slept (except for afternoon naps) and was forced to stand for hours in a hot kitchen, with only a cappuccino and a few cups of espresso to keep me awake. All of this I did for you, so that I could bring you the following recipe for *Pasta con le Sarde*, directly from its point of origin.

Luckily for all of us, Chef Angelo Pumilia at La Foresteria (part of the Planeta winery in Menfi, Sicily) took pity on me and agreed to teach me his family recipe, which I adapted below. It really is for you, as you will come to understand when you make it, taste it, share it with friends, and take credit for it. And with that, all of my suffering shall not have been in vain.

Serves 4–6

- 1 medium onion, finely chopped
- 1 bulb fennel, very thinly sliced, reserve the fronds for garnish
- ½ cup extra-virgin olive oil
- 4 oil-packed anchovy fillets
- 8 ounces fresh sardine fillets, or fillets from 1 pound whole sardines, cut into bite-sized pieces
- ½ cup dry Marsala, or dry white wine
- 1 teaspoon saffron
- 1 cup fish stock
- ½ cup golden raisins, coarsely chopped
- ½ cup pine nuts, toasted
- Salt to taste
- Freshly ground pepper to taste
- 1 pound bucatini or spaghetti
- ½ cup, heaping, unseasoned breadcrumbs, toasted
- ¼ cup toasted almonds, chopped—optional

Bring a large pot of salted water to a boil.

In a large skillet over medium heat, sauté the onion and fennel in the olive oil, add the anchovies and mash into a paste. When the onion is golden, add the sardines and Marsala wine and cook for two minutes. Dissolve saffron in the fish stock—if you don't have fish stock, you can substitute with water—and add to the skillet. Add the raisins, toasted pine nuts, and salt and pepper and cook for five minutes.

Cook the pasta until *al dente* (about 2 minutes less than package directions), drain, reserve 1 cup of the cooking water, and add the pasta to the sardines. Toss together and cook for an additional minute or so—add reserved cooking water if the pasta seems too dry.

Garnish with breadcrumbs, almonds, chopped fennel fronds to serve.

Serve immediately.

VINO

Bianco: Carricante or Verdicchio
Rosato: Syrah

This savory-sweet recipe calls for a bone-dry wine with mineral high notes and fruit undertones. The Carricante grape is grown almost exclusively on Mount Etna. These wines favor stony, gunflint notes with stone fruits vaguely noticeable in the background. In a pinch, look for a Verdicchio from the Marche. In the rosato category, look for a Syrah, known for its cracked black pepper notes that will nicely counter the sweetness of the raisins and Marsala.

SPAGHETTI AGLIO OLIO E PEPERONCINO

Spaghetti with Garlic, Chili Peppers, and Olive Oil

What's boring, gray, and has a thousand crow's feet? That's right: my 25th class reunion at Colgate University. No, seriously, everyone looked incredibly well preserved (Botox), was in great shape (Spanx), and was in a terrific mood (Xanax). They wore the latest fashions (from New Canaan) and drove the coolest cars (SUVs). It was wonderful to meet the spouses (none came) and to talk about their exciting lives (travel soccer). They exercised vigorously (12 holes of golf with gin and tonics) and danced to the latest tunes (jumped up and down in front of a Dead band). And boy did they laugh (medicinal marijuana) and eat the finest foods (chicken wings). It was great to rekindle old friendships (kegs of beer). I can't wait to see everyone again soon. (I'm good for five years.)

And then there was my friend from San Francisco, who shall remain anonymous, (Susie K.), who told me that she loved reading *Sunday Pasta*, but asked if I could make it easier for her. (I have witnesses.) Susie, this recipe is for you: 4 ingredients, 15 minutes. Happy now?

This recipe is doubly appropriate because it is the first choice for late night eating Italy. Called a *spaghettata*, it is whipped up for a group of friends of all ages after a night out.

Serves 4–6

- ½ cup extra virgin olive oil
- 2 cloves garlic, finely chopped
- 2 hot chili peppers, seeded and minced, or crushed red pepper
- 1 pound spaghetti
- Salt to taste

Bring a large pot of salted water to a boil.

Add the olive oil to a large skillet over medium heat. When the oil is hot, add the garlic and the pepper. Mix together, lower the heat and cook until garlic is golden. Remove from the heat. Cook the spaghetti until *al dente* (about 2 minutes less than package directions), drain and add it to the skillet. Cook together for 30 seconds. Add salt to taste.

Serve immediately.

VINO

Rosso: Lambrusco (Dry)

Lambrusco is a favorite, easy-sipping Italian wine. Dry, refreshing, deeply-colored and lightly tannic, its effervescence and youthful fruit give it charm, and its deep color lends a hint of mystery. Lambrusco shows purple and blue fruit along with a sottobosco (underbrush) note. It's complex yet simple and perfect, all at the same time! While the rosé and white versions are easy sippers, it is best to switch to red for dining.

ORECCHIETTE CON RAPINI E SALSICCIA

Orecchiette with Broccoli Rabe and Sausage

She's on the endangered species list. Maybe only a few hundred thousand left. Average age around 75, probably lost her mate, generally in a black coat, prominent proboscis, and a few errant whiskers. At full maturity, her arms match the strength and diameter of a body builder. By day, she gathers and prepares food for her young. A social animal, she spends hours interacting with her kind. Her lair is as clean as it gets. Dirt and disorder are her natural enemies.

Tragically, almost extinct, The Southern Italian Grandmother is among the proud few with the skill and patience necessary to churn out hundreds of quarter sized orecchiette, by hand, before mealtime. Although sightings are rare, if you're lucky, she'll emerge from her den to shape them while sitting in front of it. Just don't touch, or you'll get whacked with a wooden spoon faster than you can blink an eye.

Give today to "Save the Nonna." The world's culinary pleasure depends on it.

Serves 4–6

- 1 pound broccoli rabe
- 12 ounces sweet Italian sausage, removed from casing
- ¼ cup olive oil
- 2 cloves garlic, finely chopped
- 1 small chili pepper, finely chopped
- Salt to taste
- 1 pound orecchiette
- Grated Pecorino Romano

Bring a large pot of salted water to a boil.

Wash the broccoli rabe, removing the tough stems and large leaves, and cut it into two inch sections. Cook the broccoli rabe in the boiling water for a few minutes until it's tender but not soft. Use a wire mesh strainer to remove the broccoli rabe from the pot. Reserve the water for the pasta.

In a large skillet over medium heat, add the olive oil, garlic, and chili pepper. When the garlic is golden, crumble the sausage into the skillet. When it's browned, add the broccoli rabe and salt to taste.

Bring the broccoli rabe water back to a boil.

Cook the pasta until *al dente* (about 2 minutes less than package directions). Drain, and add to the sausage and broccoli rabe mixture.

Serve with grated Pecorino.

VINO

Bianco: Verdeca or Sauvignon Blanc
Rosso: Primitivo

Broccoli rabe has bitterness, so wines with a touch of tannin work nicely. Puglia's native grapes can pair well. The white Verdeca is typically unassuming, yet when well-made, it is fragrant, like the broccoli rabe, and has enough body and mouth-coating extract to match this dish. If you can't find Verdeca, try Sauvignon Blanc. To counter-balance the fat of the sausage while accompanying the broccoli rabe's bitterness, the light tannic grip of Primitivo red also works.

TORTELLINI ALLA PANNA CON PISELLI
Tortellini with Cream and Peas

They say that the shape of tortellini was inspired by Venus' navel, which was so beautiful that a chef in Emilia-Romagna created the pasta in its image. According to legend, he spied her belly button through the keyhole of a country inn. And that was all he could see. My, how times have changed! If Venus were alive today, odds are that her belly button would be pierced and on public display. She'd probably have a few tattoos too. Personally, I remain in the small minority that has been neither pierced nor tattooed. When asked if he would ever get a tattoo, my brother Philip simply replied: "Would you put a bumper sticker on a Ferrari?"

Inspired by the goddess of love herself, tortellini are delicious in tomato sauce, broth, cream—really in any sauce. So quit navel gazing, and go make yourself a bowl of *tortellini alla panna!*

Serves 4–6

2 tablespoons butter

1 cup heavy cream

½ cup grated Parmigiano

8 ounces peas, thawed if frozen

Salt to taste

Freshly ground white pepper to taste

1 pound tortellini

Note: I use fresh tortellini with meat, but cheese or any filling will work.

In a large skillet over medium heat melt butter, add the cream and Parmigiano, stirring constantly until the cream is reduced in half. Add the peas to the cream sauce.

Remove from heat and set aside.

Cook the tortellini until *al dente* (about 2 minutes less than package directions). Reheat the cream mixture, and use a [wire-mesh] strainer to remove tortellini from the pot into skillet with cream and peas. Cook for 1–2 minutes. If the mixture seems too thick, add a tablespoon or two of the pasta water.

Serve immediately.

VINO

Frizzante: Pignoletto or Verdicchio Frizzante

Bianco: Pignoletto or Verdicchio

Rosso: Negrettino or Sangiovese di Romagna

A dish typical of Emilia Romagna, the butter, heavy cream, and Parmigiano Reggiano create richness here, but the peas lift the entire dish and add a garden-green note. Medium-bodied wines or those just a touch lighter will work best, as will those with herbal top notes. For white wines, which work a bit better here than reds, a Pignoletto will do well. In the red category, try Negrettino or Sangiovese di Romagna, a slightly more herbal wine than its Tuscan cousin.

SUMMER RECIPES

SPAGHETTI CON LE VONGOLE
Spaghetti with Clams

Other than the deathly allergic, who among us doesn't love a delicious bowl of spaghetti with clams? Fresh clams, garlic, parsley, olive oil. You crave; it delivers.

Imagine this perfect day. You start off with some fresh *mozzarella di bufala*, ripe tomato, just picked basil, and a drizzle of extra virgin olive oil. You can still smell the bread as it came from the oven; the thought of its crust makes your mouth water. Perhaps a slice of prosciutto is draped nearby. Someone pours you a bottomless glass of Pinot Grigio. You are surrounded and served by beautiful people. You laugh with a good friend. Puccini is in the background. In the foreground, sailboats bobble as you look over a cliff onto the deep blue Tyrrhenian Sea. A cool breeze blows while you decide whether you still need your sunglasses. The *spaghetti alle vongole* arrives. Perfection. Ahhh, *la dolce vita*.

Now snap out of it, and just be happy that I'm giving you a good recipe that you can make at home, while your kids scream in the background and you overlook a sea of bills. Savor the taste, I tell you. It's all you've got! That, and your dreams.

Serves 4–6

3 pounds Manila clams, well-scrubbed
3 cloves garlic, chopped coarsely
1 cup olive oil
1 tablespoon chopped, flat-leaf parsley
Salt to taste
Freshly ground black pepper, to taste
1 pound spaghetti
Crushed red pepper—optional

Remove any clams that are broken, or which do not close immediately if tapped. Soak the clams in cold water for several hours in order to loosen any internal sand.

Bring a large pot of salted water to a boil.

In a large skillet over medium heat sauté the garlic in the olive oil until golden. Add the clams and cover the skillet. Cook for about 5 minutes or until the shells open—discard unopened clams. Remove the clams from the skillet with a wire-mesh strainer or slotted spoon. Remove most of them from their shells—saving a few in their shells. Place all shelled clams back into the skillet with the remaining liquid.

Cook the linguine until *al dente*. Drain, and add the pasta to the clam sauce. Add the clams in their shells as well. Cook for 2 minutes. Toss with the parsley, salt and pepper to taste.

Serve immediately. If desired, sprinkle with a little crushed red pepper for a kick.

VINO
Frizzante: Pinot Grigio
Bianco: Pinot Grigio

Clams are briny. Garlic is earthy. Parsley is leafy. Wines with minerality, earthiness and sea breeze make excellent matches. Red wines generally clash with the clams' saline qualities, and most rosatos will seem overly fruity, so stick to white sparkling and still wines. Pinot Grigio can show touches of all of these flavors along with some apple notes and nuttiness. A number of bubbly versions, more lightly sparkling than spumante, offer a glass that's a bit more festive.

CAVATAPPI CON RUCOLA E RICOTTA
Cavatappi with Arugula and Ricotta

Every time I turn around, some child or adult is being diagnosed with ADD (Attention Deficit Disorder). It's enough to make your head spin. I don't know what to believe anymore, but who's got time to think about it? I'm too busy managing my Blackberry, iPhone, iPod, iPad, laptop, desktop, Kindle, DVR, job, wife, kids, blog and five just-started books. And just today I saw on Headline News that cursive is no longer being taught in schools. I suppose there is no reason to write thank you notes when *u cn jst txt thx*. Alas, the Death of Details (ADD) is almost upon us.

But there must be some beacon of light in this whirlwind of darkness. And we can only hope that it shines from Miss Porter's School, where I'm certain that manners and details are still *de rigueur*. I mean, who needs Mandarin when you can study French? Luckily, one of their more famous Italian alumnae, Cristina QZ, writing in from SW3 2ED, has provided us with the following recipe. It's fast enough for those of us with ADD, and yet posh enough for those of us who care about ADD.

Serves 4–6

- 2 cloves garlic, finely chopped
- 3 tablespoons olive oil
- 12 ounces arugula, rinsed and dried
- 8 ounces fresh, whole milk ricotta
- ¼ cup grated Parmigiano
- Salt to taste
- Freshly ground black pepper to taste
- 1 pound cavatappi, or other tubular pasta

Bring a large pot of salted water to a boil.

In a large skillet over medium heat sauté the garlic in the olive oil until pale gold. Add most of the arugula (save a few leaves for garnish) and sauté until wilted.

Add the cooked arugula, ricotta, Parmigiano, salt and pepper to a food processor and pulse until thoroughly mixed, but not puréed.

Cook the pasta until *al dente* (about 2 minutes less than package directions), drain, and place into a serving bowl. Toss in the arugula mixture.

Serve immediately garnished with the remaining arugula.

VINO
Rosato: Cerasuolo d'Abruzzo
Rosso: Cerasuolo di Vittoria

Cerasuolo can accompany a variety of foods. So try a red Cerasuolo from Sicily or a Cerasuolo d'Abruzzo—a rosé from Abruzzo. Both versions are juicy and refreshing wine styles, plump with red cherry and raspberry fruits and accented by notes of wild flowers and dried herbs which will pair well with arugula. The Abruzzese wines should definitely be consumed chilled, like any rosato, and the Sicilian version slightly cooled.

SPAGHETTI CON POMODORO E BASILICO

Spaghetti with Tomato and Basil

a world in tatters
riots war recession 'quakes
ball of confusion

tomato basil
olive oil garlic pepper
salt parmigiano

spaghetti vino
a simple summer pleasure
escape share love

Haiku by Author

Tomato-based sauces can be remarkably seasonal, depending on the freshness of the tomatoes and how long they are cooked. The medium weight Basic Tomato Sauce found in the introduction of the book makes an excellent year round sauce. A ragú can be cooked for hours with meat, which creates a hearty winter sauce. On the other hand, the below recipe is perfect for warmer weather, as it requires less time in the kitchen and makes for a lighter dish.

Serves 4–6

2 pounds fresh paste (plum) tomatoes, rinsed, or one 28-ounce can whole, peeled plum tomatoes

3 cloves garlic, chopped

½ cup olive oil

1 teaspoon salt

1 teaspoon freshly ground pepper

12 leaves basil, coarsely chopped, plus several whole leaves for garnish

1 pound spaghetti

Grated Parmigiano

Bring a pot of water to boil. Add the tomatoes and cook for 90 seconds. Remove with a slotted spoon and place immediately into a bowl of ice water to stop them from cooking. Peel the tomatoes, cut them in half, remove the seeds, and julienne into ½-inch strips. If using canned tomatoes, add to a bowl and mash them together with your hands.

Bring another large pot of salted water to a boil.

In a large skillet, over medium heat sauté the garlic in the olive oil until it turns golden. Add the tomatoes, salt and pepper. Cook over medium heat for about 10 minutes, or until the tomatoes release their juices and begin to reduce slightly. Add the basil and cook for about 5 minutes more.

Cook the spaghetti until *al dente* (about 2 minutes less than package directions), drain, and add it to the tomatoes. Cook together for about one minute.

Serve garnished with basil leaves and grated Parmigiano.

VINO

Bianco: Soave

Frizzante: Bardolino

Rosso: Bardolino

This dish calls for light to mid-weight wines. The tomatoes need brisk acidity, and the basil needs some herbal notes. This generally suggests cooler climate wines, such as those from the Veneto. Soave is made from Garganega and sometimes a portion of Trebbiano di Soave. A blend of these grapes works nicely as the Trebbiano contributes breadth to the lean Garganega. Or, try lighter reds from Bardolino, especially ones with soft tannins that can take a light chill.

TROFIE AL PESTO GENOVESE
Trofie with Basil Pesto

I once had a bowl of *trofie al pesto* for dessert. We were young, carefree, and on the Italian Riviera, Zelda and I. We wandered into just any trattoria. The pasta arrived at the table. I can only describe it as indescribably delicious. When the chef emerged from the kitchen, I lunged to hug him as he asked if we wanted dessert. All I could say was, "Yes, *Si*, more *trofie al pesto*." He laughed and obliged.

I am always amazed by how far *Pesto Genovese* in America has strayed from its original, ideal perfection. How could something 1,200 years old and so beautiful, be so damned by one generation? Watered-down, over-salted, creamed, and mixed with chicken.

It's time for pesto's second act in America. I've gone to the Consortium of Pesto Genovese Producers in Liguria for the official recipe. Here are a few ground rules:

1. Use a marble mortar and a pestle (or a food processor on pulse mode as a second choice).
2. Don't be cheap with the ingredients. Use the freshest basil you can find. Wash it gently and pat it dry. Use Italian olive oil, cheese, and pine nuts.
3. Trofie and trenette are the preferred pasta choices.
4. Practice and enjoy the process.
5. Because you're worth it.

Serves 4–6

- 2–3 cups fresh, tender basil leaves
- 2 cloves garlic
- ½ cup extra virgin olive oil
- 6 tablespoons grated Parmigiano, plus extra for serving
- 2 tablespoons grated Pecorino Romano
- 1 tablespoon pine nuts
- Salt
- 1 pound trofie or trenette (or spaghetti)

Gently wash the basil in cold water and pat dry with a towel. Crush a clove of garlic in a mortar and add some basil (30 leaves per clove), and then a pinch of salt. Using a gentle circular motion, use the mortar to pound the basil until it turns into a bright green oily liquid. Repeat this process until all the basil and garlic are added. Add the pine nuts and gently crush them into the mixture. Add the cheese and slowly drizzle in the olive oil while mixing together. Avoid turning the sauce into a puree; it should have a fine, leafy consistency.

Bring a large pot of salted water to a boil.

Cook the pasta until *al dente* (about 2 minutes less than package directions). Drain, retain some of the cooking water, and place in a large, warm serving bowl. Slowly mix in the pesto sauce. Add some of the cooking water if the pasta seems too dry.

Serve immediately with grated Parmigiano.

VINO
Rosato: Ciliegiolo or Pinot Nero
Rosso: Rossese or Pinot Nero

The basil in this recipe maximizes flavor lift, calling for a wine that is equally aromatic. The pine nuts provide a fattiness that spreads the pasta across the palate, asking for a wine that matches its medium and rich body. This pasta hails from Liguria, so it's nice to match this pesto with local varieties, like Ciliegiolo and Rossese. Both of these local black grapes possess plenty of vibrant acidity and medium body to balance this oily dish.

MEZZA RIGATONI CON ZUCCHINE
Mezza Rigatoni with Zucchini

Why is it that most people can pronounce the word "zucchini" with relative ease but can't seem to manage a proper "bruschetta"? Believe me, this is not a mere tomato-tomahto, potato-potahto kind of thing; it's just a flat-out, widespread mispronunciation. Such a beautiful word, so savagely butchered. But rather than dwell on this particular pet peeve of mine, let's clear it up. In Italian, the letter combination "ch" is pronounced "k". Therefore, if you can pronounce zu**ch**ini, you can pronounce brus**ch**etta. Say it slowly and enjoy the melody. And the next time someone offers you "brushetta," look them straight in the eye and say, "I'm not exactly sure what that is, but I'd love a good brus**ch**etta." Eventually, everyone will catch on.

Now let's talk about zucchini and spaghetti. (And by the way, the "gh" in spaghetti is always pronounced that way.) Zucchini is a wildly popular vegetable in Italy, so as you can imagine, it gets a lot of play with all sorts of pasta. It can be fried, puréed, sautéed, and mixed with a variety of partners, ranging from other vegetables to pancetta to shrimp. I like it all ways, but sometimes I love it solo, when it's the star of the show.

Serve 4–6

- 8 small zucchini, thinly sliced—about ⅛ inch or less
- Olive oil for frying
- Salt to taste
- 1 small onion, finely chopped
- 1 pound mezza rigatoni (or spaghetti)
- Freshly ground black pepper to taste
- Grated Parmigiano

Divide the sliced zucchini in half.

In a large skillet, over medium-high heat, with at least ¼ inch of olive oil, fry half of the zucchini until golden brown. You may need to do this in two or more batches, but don't be lazy; you want them crispy. Place on paper towels to drain, and keep warm. Lightly sprinkle with salt (and try not to eat them). In the same skillet, add the remaining olive oil and onion, and sauté until translucent. Add the remaining zucchini and sauté until softened, or lightly browned. Add salt and pepper to taste.

Bring a large pot of salted water to a boil.

Cook the spaghetti until al dente (about 2 minutes less than the package directions), drain, and retain a cup of the cooking water. Add the pasta to the skillet with the zucchini and about half of the fried pieces, mix for 1 minute over a medium heat and add the retained pasta water to loosen the sauce.

Serve, garnished with the remaining pieces of fried zucchini and grated Parmigiano.

VINO

Bianco: Trebbiano
Rosso: Vernatsch, a.k.a. Schiava

Zucchini tastes green and earthy, showing freshness layered over bass notes. Here it is fried, so pair it with a mid-weight wine with refreshing acidity to match the weight and counteract the fat. For a white, select a youthful Trebbiano-driven blend. Though Trebbiano is remarkable as an aged, stand-alone variety, it would over-power this dish. The red Vernatch has innate earthiness to match this dish, as well as bright blueberry fruit to contrast it.

PACCHERI CON PESCE SPADA
Paccheri with Swordfish

Ah, the Hamptons … Can't live with 'em, can't live without 'em. And by without them, I mean that *The New York Post* would be blank all summer long. Yes, I always read *The Police Blotter* first, but *Page Six* is where I get the Summer Stop and Frisk updates that I care about, all of which occur in the Hamptons after dark. Plus, *Page Six* is chock full of other globally important news. For example, just today I learned the following: Alec Baldwin blah blah blah, Christie Brinkley blah blah blah, Hedge Fund geek blah blah blah …

But where New Yorkers go, good food follows, and it's usually Italian. And so, just down the road from all of the Clinton hullabaloo, the relatively low key *Osteria Salina* serves up authentic Sicilian cuisine on a side street in Bridgehampton. If Billy Joel was dining there I didn't notice, as I couldn't take my eyes off of my bucatini with swordfish. Chef Cinzia Gaglio was kind enough to send me her recipe, which I adapted and prepared the day I got home. Here is a little bit of Sicily and the Hamptons for all of us to enjoy.

Serves 4–6

1 tablespoon finely chopped onion

3 tablespoons extra virgin olive oil

1 clove garlic, thinly sliced

1 pinch crushed red pepper

1 pound swordfish (thick filet), cubed

8 Castelvetrano olives, pitted and halved, or another meaty green olive

½ tablespoon small capers

2 cups passata di pomodoro (tomato puree)

1 tablespoon Italian flat leaf parsley, finely chopped

⅛ teaspoon freshly ground black pepper

Salt to taste

1 pound paccheri (bucatini or spaghetti)

Bring a large pot of salted water to a boil.

In a large skillet, over medium heat, sauté the onion in 2 tablespoons olive oil until lightly golden. Add the garlic and crushed red pepper and cook until golden brown.

Add swordfish and sauté until gold on all sides. Add the passata di pomodoro. (You can make the passata di pomodoro by passing canned tomatoes through a food mill.). Stir and simmer for 3 minutes over medium heat.

Add the olives, capers, and parsley to the sauce. Simmer for one minute.

Cook the pasta until *al dente* (about 2 minutes less than the package directions), drain it, and add to the skillet with the sauce. Mix together.

Serve immediately.

VINO

Bianco: Falanghina

Rosso: Lacrima di Morro d'Alba

Swordfish is meaty and works equally well with mid-weight whites and reds. Olives and capers are outliers, best matched with dry, unoaked wines. Falanghina is farmed only in Campania, where it is grown in volcanic soils that give it a smokiness that blends well with this fish preparation. The Marche's Lacrima di Morro d'Alba produces massively fragrant wines packed with wild berries, plums and roses, offering a nicely fruit-driven contrast.

LINGUINE AL LIMONE
Linguine with Lemon

Starchitects Brian Bockman and Jack Forbes were recently visiting from New Orleans. There, they design hip Garden District homes and contemplate building a bright future with Brangelina in a thriving, post-Katrina city. Here, among other things, they taught me about the hidden evil that lurks in FF&A (furnishings, fixtures, and accessories), which, if you have any taste, should cost more than the home itself. Who knew?

Jack was recently in Rome where he tried *spaghetti al limone*, and thus, this was his request for *Sunday Pasta*, chez Garrubbo. It seems a quintessential summer dish, even though it really isn't that light.

Below is the recipe, which I've made many times before. This time, however, I decided that measuring is for amateurs and went heavy on the lemon zest (a mistake) and used vodka instead of grappa (a mistake) and just dumped in the cheese (a mistake). Yes, it still tasted good, but the lesson here is that when dealing with bold flavors, bright colors, and big personalities, it's better to measure and proceed with caution.

Serves 4–6

2 lemons
½ cup grappa or 1 cup dry white wine
3 tablespoons butter
1 cup heavy cream
½ cup grated Parmigiano
Salt to taste
Freshly ground black pepper to taste
1 pound linguine

Bring a large pot of salted water to a boil.

Zest one lemon and set aside the zest. Juice two lemons and discard the pulp.

In a large saucepan over medium heat, cook the grappa (or wine) with the butter, lemon juice, and ½ of the zest. When reduced and slightly syrupy, add the cream, and salt and pepper to taste. Cook on low heat until further reduced, about 3–5 minutes.

Cook the spaghetti until *al dente* (about 2 minutes less than the package directions), drain and reserve 1 cup of the cooking water.

Add the pasta to the pan with the lemon cream sauce, and add some of the reserved pasta water if the sauce seems too dry. When mixed together, place the spaghetti in a warm serving bowl and toss in the Parmigiano.

Garnish with the remaining lemon zest, and serve immediately

VINO
Spumante: Franciacorta

The pasta is rich and hearty, yet the lemon gives it a tingling, lively acidity. This dish meshes the stark contrasts of cream and aged cheese, perfect for sparkling wines to tackle. Franciacorta sparklers are among the most elegant in Italy. In fact, these are Italy's bubblies that most closely resemble Champagne. They are made mostly from Chardonnay, Pinot Blanc and Pinot Noir grapes, the first and last of which are classic Champagne grapes.

PAPPARDELLE AL PROSCIUTTO
Pappardelle with Prosciutto

When pigs fly! Yeah, I'll tell you when pigs fly. Pigs fly every time their hind legs are cured in salt and then aged for 12–24 months in the vicinity of Parma, Italy. Pigs fly every time they are turned into prosciutto. That's right, they fly off the slicer at the speed of light and into my mouth. They fly non-stop when wrapped around a grissini breadstick into my mouth. When paired with mozzarella and red pepper or tomato, with delicious crusty bread, there is a supersonic pig flight directly into my mouth. For me, this pig flies at warp speed as often as I can get my hands on it, no matter how or when it is served. So fasten your seat belts, because if you make this *pappardelle al prosciutto* for your guests, it's going to be a bumpy night.

Serves 4–6

1 onion, diced
¼ cup olive oil
10 ounces prosciutto, thinly sliced
1 28-ounce can peeled plum tomatoes, puréed
Salt to taste
Freshly ground black pepper to taste
1 pound pappardelle, tagliatelle or fettuccine
Grated Parmigiano

In a large skillet, over medium heat, add the onion to the olive oil and sauté until golden. Add the prosciutto and stir together until fully incorporated and slightly browned—be careful not to let it get crispy. Add the tomatoes and salt and pepper. Cook for 10–15 minutes until the sauce has slightly thickened.

Bring a large pot of salted water to a boil.

Cook the pasta until *al dente* (about 2 minutes less than the package directions). Drain, and add to the prosciutto mixture.

Serve with grated Parmigiano.

VINO
Rosso: Sangiovese di Romagna

Sangiovese di Romagna tends to be lighter in color and weight than Sangiovese di Toscana. It shows generous, fresh herb notes, and sometimes its tannins can be less ripe and a bit more edgy. It is a nice match with this pasta as long as the tannins are ripe and the acidity is balanced.

FUSILLI ALLA CHECCA

Fusilli with Tomato and Mozzarella

Once again, I was in an interminable, unnatural, and indecent bind. I did not enjoy the pain. Soft music played in the background as a soft voice commanded me to focus. Yes, this was yoga class. I thought to myself, "But I am focusing … on pasta. That's better than thinking about work, right?" My mind raced from pasta to pasta to pasta. "Why shouldn't these positions be named after pasta instead of animals? How much nicer would it be to move into "farfalle" instead of crow and to settle into "fettuccine" instead of pigeon? Nice idea, I thought, but in the end, they're all just fusilli to me—and that would make it even more boring.

But as proof that misery often brings clarity, today we eat fusilli! Call it what you will, but its twists, curves, and contortions make it flexible enough to complement almost any sauce: tomato, pesto, cream, cheese, seafood, or meat—it's all good with fusilli. On a warm summer afternoon, fusilli with barely cooked garden fresh tomato and creamy mozzarella is pure pleasure. All gain; no pain.

Namaste.

Serves 4–6

- 2 pounds plum tomatoes
- 1 large ball fresh mozzarella, coarsely chopped
- ½ cup olive oil
- ¼ cup chopped fresh basil
- 1 teaspoon salt
- ½ teaspoon freshly ground black pepper
- 1 red onion, thinly sliced (optional)
- Grated Parmigiano

Bring a large pot of water to boil. Add the tomatoes and cook for 90 seconds. Remove them to a bowl of ice water to stop the cooking. Peel, seed and cut them into bite-size pieces. Set aside.

Bring a large pot of salted water to a boil.

In a large bowl, add the mozzarella, ¼ cup olive oil, basil, parsley, salt and pepper, and mix together.

Cook the pasta until *al dente* (about 2 minutes less than the package directions).

In a skillet over medium heat, sauté the onion in ¼ cup olive oil. Add the tomatoes when the onion begins to turn golden and stir. Cook 10 minutes, or until the pasta is done.

Drain the pasta and add to the serving bowl with the mozzarella. Stir in the tomato mixture and serve immediately, with grated Parmigiano.

Note: In Rome, it would be common to use raw tomatoes for this recipe, offering an even lighter taste. In this case, simply chop the tomatoes, or use cherry tomatoes cut into halves, and mix them with the mozzarella prior to adding the pasta to serving bowl. One might also substitute caciotta cheese for the Parmigiano.

VINO

Spumante: Franciacorta Pinot Nero
Rosso: Ciliegiolo

For this dish, wines with aromatic pop and no new oak exposure work best. As this is a mid-weight pasta, try a lighter and higher acid wine. For a still wine, try a medium-bodied, softly tannic and fruit-driven wine from Ciliegiolo, which is a little heralded grape historically used in Chianti blends. For a sparkling wine, Pinot Nero's red fruit notes will combine seamlessly with the substantial ripeness of late summer tomatoes.

RIGATONI ALLA NORMA
Rigatoni with Eggplant

So dark, so bitter, so misunderstood. So Sicilian. Ok, enough about me. Let's talk about eggplant which, like me, is an acquired taste.

As I watch my children gag over eggplant, I recall my own such repulsion as a child. Why and when eggplant became delicious to me is somewhat of a blur, but if I recall, the moment involved both rigatoni and olive oil. Although she didn't call it Norma, my grandmother regularly whipped up this Sicilian classic. In retrospect, it tied well into my grandfather's passion for opera, as the dish is probably named after Vincenzo Bellini's opera "Norma". (It was supposedly named so by the Sicilian writer Nino Martoglio, who was so impressed by the dish that he compared it to the opera.)

Call it *pasta alla melanzana* if you prefer, and use penne or spaghetti if you please. With one taste, you will understand that this dish is neither dark nor bitter at all (like me, generally).

Serves 4–6

- 2 medium eggplants, washed and cut into ¼-inch rounds
- 1 onion, finely chopped
- ½ cup olive oil for the sauce, plus more for frying the eggplant
- 1 28-ounce can plum tomatoes, puréed
- 1 teaspoon salt, plus more for salting the eggplant
- 1 teaspoon freshly ground black pepper
- 6 ounces ricotta salata, grated
- 1 pound rigatoni
- Basil leaves for garnish

Sprinkle both sides of the eggplant with salt and place in a colander. Cover with paper towels and a heavy object such as another can, or two, of tomatoes. Let stand for an hour to allow the bitterness to drain out of the eggplant.

In a large skillet over medium heat sauté the onion in ¼ cup olive oil until the onion is golden. Add the tomatoes, salt and pepper, lower the heat and cook until reduced by about a third. In another pan, fry the eggplant in up to 1 inch of olive oil until golden. As an alternative, coat the eggplant in olive oil and bake in a 400°F oven until golden, making sure to turn regularly. Either way, place the fried eggplant on paper towels to drain and keep warm.

Bring a large pot of salted water to a boil.

Cook the rigatoni until *al dente* (about 2 minutes less than the package directions), drain, and add to a large serving bowl. Add a ladle of sauce and mix in ½ of the grated ricotta.

Serve immediately in individual bowls, covered with more sauce and 4–5 pieces of eggplant. Top with the remaining ricotta and a basil leaf.

VINO

Rosso: Nerello Mascalese Blends

Even in a bright tomato sauce, the eggplant rules the wine pairing and its meatiness insists on red wine. Nerello Mascalese is a grape indigenous to Sicily's northeast corner. It is produced on Mount Etna and the surrounding area on the island's northeast tip. Its mineral, gamey character is a tasty match for this recipe. Nerello Mascalese isn't short on tannins, so it is often blended with other grapes to soften the wine. These wines are usually higher in alcohol too, making them just the right weight for this robust pasta.

GNUDI DI SPINACI E RICOTTA
Spinach and Ricotta Gnudi

Let's discuss weighty matters. Nah, forget it. Let's just get naked. Or, we could do both. With *gnudi*.

Gnocchi is a general term for "dumplings" in Italian, usually referring to the most popular type, made with potato. Many people incorrectly perceive gnocchi as dense and heavy, but real, Italian, handmade gnocchi are light and fluffy. And gnudi are even lighter. Gnudi is an alternative term for gnocchi in Tuscany, where they are often made with ricotta and without potato. (Gnudi are also sometimes called "naked ravioli," since they are essentially the filling without the pasta cover or because the word *gnudi* sounds like *nudi*, or naked in Italian.)

In summary, bad gnocchi are heavy and dense, good gnocchi are light and fluffy, and gnudi are their beautiful and svelte Tuscan cousins. Now, enough talk, let's get *gnudi*.

Serves 4–6

- 1 pound fresh spinach, tough stems removed, thoroughly rinsed, cook until wilted, and squeezed dry
- 10 ounces ricotta
- ½ cup grated Parmigiano
- 2 eggs
- 1 cup flour plus some to cover the gnudi
- 1 teaspoon ground nutmeg
- 1 teaspoon salt
- ½ cup butter
- 6–8 sage leaves

Place the cooked spinach in a large bowl with the ricotta, eggs and Parmigiano and mix together. Add the flour, nutmeg and salt and mix to thoroughly combine the ingredients.

Bring a large pot of salted water to a boil.

Cover a cutting board or counter top with flour. Use two teaspoons to form small balls with the spinach mixture and roll in the flour. When all the mixture has been made into balls, place several at a time into the boiling water and cook until they begin to float, 2–3 minutes. Remove with a slotted spoon, and place on a serving dish.

In a small skillet, over low heat, melt the butter with the sage. Pour over the gnudi.

Serve immediately with grated Parmigiano.

VINO

Bianco: Soave
Rosso: Bardolino

The dominant ingredients of this dish are spinach and sage. Wines offering herbal top notes will blend well. Cool climate wines with refreshing, even searing acidity work to revive the palate from the dish's dairy elements. The Veneto has several options, including Garganega—the base of Soave, and Bardolino blends—made from the Corvina, Rondinella and Molinara grapes.

TAGLIATELLE CON RADICCHIO E SPECK
Tagliatelle with Radicchio and Speck

When most people think of Germany, they think Autobahn, engineering, and Oktoberfest. I, however, think immediately of my favorite Teutonic Titwillow, Lili von Shtupp (as played by the immortal Madeline Kahn) in *Blazing Saddles*. She remains emblazoned on my mind when it comes to all things Germanic. It's twue. It's twue…

Which brings me to *speck*, a favorite ham from Trentino-Alto Adige, the far northern province of Italy. Bordered by Austria and Switzerland, it has bounced back and forth between German, Austrian, and Italian control and culture over the centuries. Today, the area is officially Italian, even though Alto Adige is still called South Tyrol in English and Germanic influences and language are omnipresent. Speck is the region's version of prosciutto, seasoned differently than its famous Parma counterpart.

Like many bitter foods, radicchio mellows in intensity when cooked, especially with onion. For a more intense flavor, you can skip the cream. Either way, it's a perfect dish. Really, it's twue.

Serves 4–6

1 onion, finely chopped
2 tablespoons olive oil
6 ounces speck, cut into bite-sized strips or cubes
1 head of radicchio, cored and sliced into medium strips
¾ cup heavy cream
½ cup white wine
Salt to taste
Freshly ground black pepper to taste
1 pound tagliatelle
Grated Parmigiano

Bring a large pot of salted water to boil.

In a large skillet over medium heat, sauté the onion in the olive oil until translucent. Add the speck and sauté until browned, careful not to let it get crispy. Add the radicchio and cook until it wilts. Add the wine and stir together until it evaporates. Add the cream, salt and pepper to taste, and cook until the sauce begins to reduce, 3–5 minutes.

Cook the pasta until *al dente* (about 2 minutes less than the package directions), drain and add to the radicchio mixture.

Serve with grated Parmigiano.

VINO

Bianco: Gewürztraminer
Rosso: Lagrein or Pinot Nero

The strategy here is to match the radicchio's bitterness in the white category and counter it in the red. In either color, the wine should be fairly full in body—at least 13.5% alcohol. Aromatic white varieties like Gewürztraminer and Muscat can exhibit light bitter notes when vinified completely dry, working perfectly with this pasta. Alternatively, choose reds with smooth tannins or good fruit plumpness to buffer the tannins, like Pinot Nero or Lagrein.

BUCATINI CACIO E PEPE
Bucatini with Cheese and Black Pepper

Meet my friends, Cacio and Pepe. Cacio is pale white, from the countryside outside of Rome. Pepe is black as night, of mysterious origins. Their relationship is still taboo in most of America. As a matter of fact, I've never seen them together outside of New York (where there is a restaurant named in their honor). If they ever were to make it down South, who knows what the reaction would be … Oh my!

Actually, this should come as no surprise because one in the relationship is very salty and the other very peppery, and together, they can be downright explosive—a real shock to the senses for the unfamiliar. Now in Rome, where minds are more open, Cacio and Pepe can be found on almost every corner, like Dolce & Gabbana. Usually seen with their friends, Spaghetti and Tonnarelli, they make everyone happy. We can only hope that someday Cacio and Pepe will be fully accepted in America.

Serves 4–6

1 tablespoon olive oil

1 cup grated Pecorino Romano cheese

2 tablespoons coarsely ground black pepper

1 pound bucatini (or spaghetti)

Bring a large pot of salted water to boil.

Coat the bottom of a large skillet with the olive oil.

Add the Pecorino to a bowl.

Cook the pasta until *al dente* (about 2 minutes less than the package directions). While it's cooking, take 3–4 tablespoons of the water and mix into the Pecorino, creating a creamy mixture. Stir in the pepper. Drain the pasta and reserve some of the cooking water. Add the pasta to the oiled skillet over low heat, making sure not to fry the spaghetti, but rather only to coat it with oil. Mix in the cheese and pepper, and add a bit more of the reserved cooking water, as necessary, until a creamy consistency is achieved.

Serve immediately. Add more pepper to taste.

Note: You may need to practice a couple of times to get the right mixture and consistency. Also, Caveat Cheese Emptor: the word cacio is used for cheese in Lazio, so be aware that the brand Cacio de Roma is not what you need, despite its name. Use a good Pecorino Romano, freshly grated.

VINO

Bianco: Grechetto
Rosso: Chianti Classico

Cacio e Pepe is a mid-weight dish that calls for a medium-bodied wine. Its peppery spiciness works well with either whites or reds showing subtle fruit flavors but strong minerality. Umbria's Orvieto, a blend of the local Grechetto with Procanico (a.k.a. Trebbiano Toscano) has an underlying earthiness to match the pasta and cheese. Chianti Classico's Sangiovese dominant blends offer bright red cherry notes to contrast the simple savoriness of the pasta.

FALL RECIPES

PACCHERI CON SALSICCIA, ZUCCHINE E BURRATA

Paccheri with Sausage, Zucchini, and Burrata

Everyone knows that The David (Il Davide) is a masterpiece created by the 26-year-old artistic genius Michelangelo in 1504. The long lines to get into the *Accademia* in Florence are worth the wait to the see the 17-foot-tall sculpture, carved by hand, out of a single block of white Carrera marble. If you cannot get tickets to see the original sculpture, you can always see a replica, installed by the city in 1910 in the same location as the original once was, the Piazza della Signoria. The replica doesn't deliver nearly the same breathtaking punch of the original, but you'll get the idea.

When in Florence, it's impossible not to think of all the artistic genius that emanates from the city, including the culinary. For example, on my last visit, I ate a spectacular version of this dish at *Il Francescano*, just off the Piazza Santa Croce, alongside the Basilica containing DaVinci's bones. Odds are, it's probably not the first time or place that these particular ingredients have been artistically combined, but if the city can knock off the David, then I can copy a bowl of pasta. Not nearly as good as the original, but you'll get the idea.

Serves 4–6

- 1 pound sweet Italian sausage, casings removed, crumbled
- ¼ cup olive oil
- 1 onion, diced
- 1 large zucchini, cubed
- Salt to taste
- Freshly ground black pepper to taste
- 1 pound paccheri, or rigatoni
- 1 burrata, or mozzarella, sliced
- Grated Parmigiano

In a large skillet, over medium heat, sauté the sausage in the olive oil and add the onion. Add a bit more olive oil if the mixture seems too dry. When the onion is translucent, add the zucchini, and cook until the mixture is golden brown. Add salt and pepper.

Bring a large pot of salted water to a boil.

Cook the pasta until *al dente* (about 2 minutes less than the package directions). Drain and retain 1 cup of the cooking water. Add the pasta to the sausage mixture and thoroughly mix together over medium heat. Add some pasta water if the mixture seems too dry. Distribute the pasta into serving bowls, and top each one with a slice of burrata.

Serve immediately with Parmigiano

VINO

Bianco: Falanghina
Rosso: Vino Nobile di Montepulciano

Sausage begs for red, but with zucchini and mozzarella in the mix, richer whites work, too. Whether red or white, skip wines showing obvious oak overtones. Medium-plus bodied whites, like Campania's Falanghina, are a solid match. For reds, Vino Nobile di Montepulciano and its younger sibling Rosso di Montepulciano offer enough acidity to cut through the dish's fat.

ORECCHIETTE CON CECI

Orecchiette with Chickpeas

My birthday is fast approaching and so my mother has already brought over my annual gift bag. (For her, a gift is late if it isn't two weeks early.) The goodie bag included the usual Mass card which assures that hundreds of nuns will pray for me every Sunday for the next year. In addition, this year there was a t-shirt that reads, "Smart, good looking, and Italian, it just doesn't get any better than this." I'm sure that it's standard issue for all Italian mothers.

Is it any wonder that the average Italian male lives at home until the age of 35?

Of course, most cubs eventually do leave the den, and when they do, they are prepared to take on the world. By "prepared," I'm not suggesting any sort of domestic or emotional skills, but rather only the ability to feed themselves well. The following recipe, along with some basic training, will allow the average good looking, smart, Italian male to survive without mamma in this cruel world. It really doesn't get any better than this.

Serves 4–6

- 1 small onion, chopped
- ¼ cup olive oil
- 6 ounces pancetta, diced
- 12 ounces spinach
- 16 ounces chickpeas—if from a can, well rinsed. If dried, see below.
- Salt to taste
- Freshly ground pepper to taste
- 1 pound orecchiette, or conchiglie
- Grated Parmigiano

If using dried chick peas, soak them overnight in abundant water. In the morning, drain them, add to a large saucepan, and cover with fresh water that clears them by a few inches. Gently boil over medium-low heat for 2 hours or until tender but not mushy. Drain and reserve until needed for pasta.

In a large skillet over medium heat, sauté the onion in the olive oil for 2 minutes. Add the pancetta and cook together until the ingredients are light golden. Add the spinach and cook until wilted. Add the chickpeas, salt and pepper to taste.

Bring a large pot of salted water to a boil.

Cook the pasta until *al dente* (about 2 minutes less than the package directions), drain, and reserve 1 cup of the cooking water. Add the pasta and its water to the chickpea mixture and cook for one minute.

Serve with grated Parmigiano.

VINO

Bianco: Fiano
Rosso: Teroldego

The decadent density of this dish calls for medium-plus bodied wines. Its rich flavors can be complemented by wines showing a neutral fruit character or contrasted by wines with a vibrant fruit exuberance. The Fiano grape has the texture density to match the chickpeas while Trentino's Teroldego offers zinging acidity backed by lightly tugging tannins. These keep the palate primed by adding a generous fruit character to compensate for the chickpeas' earthiness.

PENNONE AL GORGONZOLA

Pennone with Gorganzola

I have a soft spot in my heart for gorgonzola cheese. It makes me chuckle too. All because of my Grandfather Filippo Garrubbo. Born in the USA in 1908, his parents longed for Italy and so returned there just a few years later. Shortly thereafter, his father, older brother, and uncle were killed in a quarry explosion while my grandfather was sent on an errand to buy cigarettes. This tragedy made him into the gentlest of souls. I suppose this is why he felt compelled at age 75 to tell me about what he called his life's most cruel behavior, some 50 years earlier.

You see, when he eventually returned to America as a teenager, he took a young woman on a date to the movies. He leaned over to kiss her and immediately noticed that her breath was terrible. So bad, in fact, that he excused himself to the bathroom and never returned. "She was such a nice girl," he told me with his thick accent, "but her breath smelled like a gorgonzola cheese." And now, some 75 years after that fateful date, I cannot think of gorgonzola cheese—or smell bad breath for that matter—without smiling and thinking of my grandfather.

So in his honor, please enjoy this fragrant dish. And bring breath mints for your guests.

Serves 4–6

½ cup heavy cream

2 tablespoons butter

4 ounces fontina, grated or diced

4 ounces mascarpone

4 ounces grated Parmigiano plus extra for serving

4 ounces gorgonzola dolce, diced or crumbled

1 pound pennone rigate

Salt to taste

Freshly ground black pepper to taste

Bring a large pot of salted water to a boil.

In a large skillet over medium heat, add the butter and heavy cream. When the butter is melted, add the fontina, mascarpone, Parmigiano, and gorgonzola. Stir until melted together.

Cook the pasta until *al dente* (about 2 minutes less than the package directions). Drain and add to the sauce. Cook for 1 minute, stirring until pasta is thoroughly coated.

Serve in warm bowls with grated Parmigiano, salt and pepper to taste.

VINO

Frizzante: Rosato

Rosso: Amarone

The wines for this creamy pasta will need high acidity and bright red fruit flavors to contrast the cheese's unctuousness. The dish's velvety texture can be either contrasted—with sparkling wine, or matched—with a dried grape wine. Rosato sparklers are made at least in part from black grapes, so they have red fruit flavors. Reds made from dried grapes, like Amarone, are intensely concentrated both in their flavors and in their acidity.

SPAGHETTI AL FINOCCHIO
Spaghetti with Fennel

Now that the eternally long wait is finally over, I can rest easy knowing that England has a new future king. Don't get me wrong. I'm all for the royals; my tax dollars don't pay for them and besides, they keep the news so fresh and exciting! What a fortunate coincidence, therefore, that this recipe is a perfect baby gift for both Kate and Will, as well as new parents everywhere.

You see, it's a little known fact, but fennel is thought to be a galactagogue. That's right, a galactagogue! In other words, fennel helps breastfeeding mothers improve their milk supply. You're welcome, Kate! And Will, as every man knows, hallucinogens are an important part of any new father's diet. Luckily, fennel is a key ingredient in absinthe, the once banned psychotropic liquor. You'll need plenty of absinthe to get you through that entire nursing period.

Tanti auguri to you both!

Serves 4–6

- 2–3 cloves garlic, thinly sliced
- ½ cup olive oil
- 2–3 fennel bulbs, rinsed, bottoms, tops, and tough outer layers removed, thinly sliced, length-wise
- 1 cup water
- 6 anchovy filets—optional
- ½ cup unseasoned bread crumbs—optional
- Salt to taste
- Black pepper to taste
- 1 pound spaghetti or bucatini
- Grated Parmigiano—optional

In a large skillet, over medium heat sauté the garlic in the olive oil until golden. Add the fennel and cook for 5 minutes. Add a cup of water and cook over low heat, covered, for about 15–20 minutes tender. Remove the lid and raise the heat. Sauté until the excess water evaporates and the fennel turns golden. Keep warm.

Bring a large pot of salted water to a boil.

In alternate preparation—which adds salty flavor and texture—add a tablespoon of olive oil and a clove of sliced garlic to another skillet over medium heat. When the garlic turns golden, add the anchovies, and heat together, stirring occasionally, until dissolved. Add the breadcrumbs and cook together for a minute or two until slightly toasted.

Add the pasta and cook until *al dente* (about 2 minutes less than the package directions), drain, and add to the skillet with the fennel. Cook together for a minute. If opting for the anchovies and breadcrumbs, mix in at this point.

Serve immediately. If not using the anchovy mixture, sprinkle with Parmigiano.

VINO

Bianco: Kerner or Silvaner
Rosso: Grignolino

The best pairings for this pasta need enough aromatic punch to match the recipe's fennel, so light—to medium-body wines work best. Northern Italian wines are particularly well-suited to handle this match, especially the lesser-known grape varieties Kerner and Silvaner. Alternatively, select the pale-colored but equally aromatic Grignolino, which boasts fragrances of cranberries, red plums and cloves.

CAVATELLI CON BROCCOLI

Cavatelli with Broccoli

"So we beat on, boats against the current, borne ceaselessly into the past." Frankly, I am not sure that the story is really a tragedy. Other than his untimely death, Jay seemed to be doing just fine for himself. As I sat there watching Leonardo DiCaprio play Jay Gatsby, all I could think was that this had to be the easiest gig of his career. How much of a stretch could it be for Leo to play a rich, champagne-sipping mogul, surrounded by lovely young ladies out in a Long Island mansion? I'll admit that I've never been a good judge of acting skills, but to me, Leo playing Jay was really just Leo playing Leo, except in a pink suit. Believe me, Leo is no master of disguise. Nope, the wardrobe didn't fool me.

But I'll tell you what is a true master of disguise, and that is cavatelli, which can cover the past of any vegetable. If you like broccoli, you will like it even more with cavatelli. If you don't like broccoli, you'll barely know it's there. It's the best way that I know of to get spoiled kids of all ages to eat their veggies.

Serves 4–6

- 5 cloves of garlic, sliced
- ½ cup olive oil
- 2 cups chicken broth
- Florets from 4–6 large stalks of broccoli, chopped
- 1 teaspoon salt
- 1 teaspoon freshly ground black pepper
- Crushed red pepper to taste
- 1 pound cavatelli—frozen is fine if fresh are not available
- Grated Parmigiano

In a large skillet, over medium heat, sauté the garlic in the olive oil until golden.

Bring a large pot of salted water to a boil.

Add the chicken broth carefully to the garlic so that it doesn't splatter (when it's combined with the oil). When the broth is hot, add the broccoli, cover, and cook until tender, 5–10 minutes, but not soft (so that the broccoli retains its bright green color and does not become mushy or fall apart). Add about 1 teaspoon each of salt, black pepper and/or crushed red pepper, depending on your taste.

Cook the cavatelli until *al dente* (about 1 minute less than the package directions) and drain. Add to the broccoli and toss to combine.

Serve immediately with grated Parmigiano.

Note: You can also make this into more of a soupy dish by adding extra broth. It is best eaten with a spoon, regardless of how much broth you add.

VINO

Bianco: Sauvignon Blanc
Rosso: Primitivo Blends

Pairing wine with broccoli is an unenviable chore because of the vegetable's earthy, grassy, green flavors. Stick to mid-weight wines with mouth-watering acidity. Sauvignon Blanc is perfect for broccoli, especially those wines that have spent some time in older oak. Unoaked Primitivo from Puglia has solid acidity and mild tannins that also play well with the light bitterness of the broccoli.

PENNE INTEGRALE CON CAVOLINI DI BRUXELLES

Whole Wheat Penne with Brussels Sprouts

Tastes great, less filling. The breakfast of champions. Low in calories. Rich in antioxidants. Part of a healthy diet. A good source of fiber. Helps support regularity. Supports brain function. Heart healthy. You deserve a break today. No artificial flavors or coloring. No additives or preservatives. Low in sugar. Low in fat. Got sprouts? I can't believe I ate the whole thing. I can't believe it's not butter. Where's the beef? Clap on. Clap off.

P.S. Call me crazy, but I might sometimes add a handful of pancetta and/or breadcrumbs to the dish, as they might do in Italy, where everyone seems to be healthy and svelte, mainly because they would eat this delicious bowl of whole wheat pasta and fresh vegetables without thinking twice about the above bulls–t.

Serves 4–6

- 1 pound Brussels sprouts
- 3 cloves garlic, finely chopped
- ½ cup olive oil
- Salt to taste
- Freshly ground black pepper to taste
- 1 pound whole wheat penne or spaghetti
- Grated Parmigiano

Remove the rough outer leaves of the Brussels sprouts, slice off the bottoms, and cut them in half. Thoroughly rinse. Steam for 10 minutes.

In a large pan over medium heat, sauté the garlic in the olive oil until it's golden. Add the Brussels sprouts and cover. Cook for 10 minutes, stirring frequently. Add salt and pepper to taste.

Bring a large pot of salted water to boil.

Cook the pasta until al dente (about 2 minutes less than the package directions), drain, and retain one cup of the cooking water. Add the pasta to the Brussels sprouts and mix together. Add some of the retained cooking water to achieve desired sauce consistency.

Serve with grated Parmigiano.

Note: You might like to add 6 ounces of diced pancetta to the pan, before the garlic, and cook over medium heat for a few minutes until golden and then add the garlic. Also, a handful of breadcrumbs could be added when the cooked pasta is mixed into the Brussels sprouts, for an even more savory dish.

VINO

Bianco: Grillo
Rosso: Cerasuolo

With no meat and only a grating of cheese, this is a fairly light pasta which will team best with medium-bodied wines. Sicily's Grillo can cover the white wine options. Grillo is rather neutral in flavor with some nutty undertones and dried herb top notes. In the red wine category, blends from Nero d'Avola and Frappato known as Cerasuolo produce medium-bodied reds that sometimes look as pale as rosato wines.

PENNE CON PEPERONI ARROSTO
Penne with Roasted Red Peppers

I am happy to announce that red bell peppers will soon be back in season. Full of vitamin C, lycopene and carotene, fresher and sweeter red peppers will soon be available to all of us who brave the winter. This is sort of irrelevant to me, however, since I like red peppers so much that I eat them year round, even though they may have been imported from some far-flung place. My *inconvenient truth* regarding red peppers is that after all of the growing, picking, packing, shipping, trucking, refrigerating, washing, and waxing that is required to deliver me red peppers during the winter, they probably have the carbon footprint of a minivan.

Of course, I roast the peppers myself, mainly because I've never tasted a roasted pepper from a can or a jar that is worth eating (slimy, flavorless, unidentifiable juice … in such a state that not even olive oil can save them). We keep a bottomless supply of roasted peppers at home because (like spinach) I think they are a good companion to almost any food: meat, fish, fowl, eggs, mozzarella, bread, etc. And, of course, pasta.

Serves 4–6

- 6–8 red bell peppers
- ¼ cup olive oil, plus some for drizzling
- 4 cloves garlic, finely chopped
- 1 pound pennone lisce, or other short tubular pasta
- Salt to taste
- Freshly ground black pepper to taste
- Grated Parmigiano

Heat the oven to 400° F. Cover a heavy duty baking tray with foil. Cut the peppers in half, length-wise, wash, and remove the seeds and membranes. Place the peppers, cut-side down, on the baking tray and drizzle with olive oil. Place in oven for 30–45 minutes, until the skin is dark brown or partially blackened. Remove from oven and place immediately in a metal or glass bowl, and cover with foil or a large plate. Allow the peppers to steam in the bowl for 15–30 minutes, to let the skin loosen further. Remove the skin, slice the peppers into strips, and place in another bowl. Drizzle with olive oil, some salt and pepper. Add the remaining pepper juice from the first bowl.

In a large skillet over medium heat sauté the garlic in ¼ cup olive oil until golden. Add the peppers and their juice and cook for an additional 10–15 minutes until tender but not soft.

Bring a large pot of salted water to a boil.

Cook the pasta until *al dente* (about 2 minutes less than the package directions). Drain, and add it to the skillet containing the peppers, and cook for 1 minute. Add salt and pepper to taste.

Serve with grated Parmigiano.

VINO
Rosato: Aglianico or Piedirosso

Freshly roasted red peppers have savory, smoky elements that are countered by an intense, bright sweetness. Rosé wines with the medium body swagger needed to complement this pasta hail from Italy's warmer areas, like Campania. Aglianico and Piedirosso are black grape varieties that make mineral and gamey red wines. Their rosato styles show strong spice and mineral notes that contrast nicely with the red peppers' overt sweetness.

FUSILLI CON FUNGHI, PANCETTA E PINOLI

Fusilli with Mushrooms, Pancetta, and Pine Nuts

Unlike Lincoln, I would never walk a mile to return a penny. And unlike Washington, I would never admit to cutting down a cherry tree. But there are some things about which I cannot tell a lie, and one of them is *Sunday Pasta*. So here goes. I have no idea where this recipe comes from. I know that my mamma has been making it deliciously for decades, but its origins are obscure. Maybe it hails from a quaint village in northern Italy. Or maybe, just maybe, it hails from a quaint village in northern New Jersey. Hmm…

Either way, to me it is a quintessential cool weather dish. Pinoli (pine nuts), pancetta, and fresh mushrooms combine to serve up the colors, tastes, and smells of a clear, fall day.

Serves 4–6

- 1 medium onion, finely chopped
- ⅓ cup olive oil
- 8 ounces mushrooms, any variety, cleaned and sliced
- 6 ounces pancetta, diced
- 2 tablespoons pinoli (pine nuts)
- Salt to taste
- Freshly ground black pepper to taste
- 1 pound fusilli or penne
- Grated Parmigiano

In a large skillet, over medium heat sauté the onion in the olive oil until golden. Add the mushrooms and cook until they lose their liquid and are browned. Cover and set aside.

Bring a large pot of salted water to boil.

In another skillet, over medium heat, sauté the pancetta in a little olive oil until crisp. Remove the pancetta with a slotted spoon and add to mushrooms. In the skillet where the pancetta was cooked, add the pinoli and sauté, over medium-low heat until golden brown. Add the pinoli to the mushroom and pancetta mixture. Add salt and freshly ground black pepper to taste.

Cook the pasta until *al dente* (about 2 minutes less than the package directions). Drain, and retain 1 cup of the cooking liquid. Add the pasta to the mushroom mixture and cook together for 1 minute. Add a little of the retained cooking water if the mixture seems too dry.

Serve with grated Parmigiano.

VINO

Spumante: Methodo Classico Rosato
Bianco: Vermentino

This is a savory dish, so the wines should be focused on subdued flavors like brioche, baguette and nuts. Of all wine styles, sparklers crackle most with acidity, so they are an excellent match. Alternatively, rich whites can mimic the dish's broadness on the palate. Whites with a hint of oak and unctuousness complement this pasta beautifully, if differently. Try a Vermentino, grown in warm Sardinia, often harvested early to retain acidity.

CONCHIGLIE CON FAGIOLI ROSSI
Conchiglie with Red Beans

Yo soy un hombre sincero
De donde crece la palma
Y antes de morirme quiero
Echar mis versos del alma

I am a truthful man
From where the palm tree grows
And before dying I want
To let out the verses of my soul

—José Martí

Well, the palm trees for me are located in Italy, not Cuba. And the verses of my soul seem to be pasta recipes, not poetry. But both could have been. My great grandfather Pasquale Ciccone left Avellino for America around 1895. For whatever reason, he landed in Haiti, where he lived for some years before making his way to New York. The only reason I know this is because my grandmother often prepared rice and red beans when I was a child. She once explained that she learned how to make the dish from her mother-in-law, who learned how to make it while living in Haiti.

I learned how to perfect a different version of rice and red beans while living in New Orleans, which also traces the dish back to Haiti. So here is the recipe for red beans, Italian style, brought to you via Naples, Haiti, New Orleans, and New York. These beans get around.

Serves: 4–6

- 1 cup dried red kidney beans, or one 15-ounce cans red kidney beans, drained
- 1 onion, finely chopped
- 1 celery stalk, diced
- 2 cloves garlic, finely chopped
- ¼ cup olive oil
- 8 ounces sweet Italian sausage, with casings removed
- Salt to taste
- Freshly ground black pepper to taste
- 1 pound conchiglie, or short tubular pasta
- Grated Parmigiano

Soak dried beans overnight in abundant water. In the morning, drain, add to a large saucepan, and cover them, plus a few inches, with fresh water. Gently boil over medium-low heat for 2 hours or until tender but not mushy. Drain and reserve until needed for pasta.

In a large skillet, over medium heat, sauté the onion, celery and garlic in the olive oil until the onion is lightly golden. Crumble the sausage into the skillet, and cook until the sausage is lightly browned. Add the beans to the sausage mixture. Cook over medium heat for 5–10 minutes, making sure that the beans do not disintegrate.

Bring a large pot of salted water to a boil.

Cook the pasta until *al dente* (about 2 minutes less than the package directions), drain, and retain 1 cup of cooking liquid. Add the pasta to the beans. If the mixture seems dry, add some of the pasta water. Add salt and pepper to taste.

Serve with grated Parmigiano.

VINO

Frizzante: Lambrusco (Dry)
Rosso: Salento Rosso Blends

Two proteins plus a carbohydrate make this a filling dish. Rosato frizzante and rosso will be the best bets. In fact, why not combine the rosato and frizzante to get Lambrusco? This way, you get a bit of tannin from the red varieties and a bit of chill for refreshment. For red, Salento Rosso is a juicy and mildly tannic red whose medium-plus body matches this pasta's weightier elements.

FETTUCCINE CON SALSA DI NOCI
Fettucine with Walnut Sauce

Nuts! Crazy good! Crazy simple! Crazy easy! Crazy delicious! In any language—Just crazy! Pazzo! सनकी! Meshugganah! Fou! Loco! dÚsachtach! Verrückt! 疯狂的! Galen! مجنون! Louco! クレイジー! That is, if you like walnuts.

This recipe for *salsa di noci*, or walnut sauce, sometimes called walnut pesto, reflects the traditional Ligurian preparation. For a slightly different taste and texture, you can substitute a half cup of either mascarpone or ricotta cheese for the milk and bread. Or, if you prefer a non-dairy version, add more olive oil when mixing the walnuts, and be sure to add more of the reserved cooking water, as described below. In Italy, this sauce is traditionally served with *pansotti* (ravioli) filled with ricotta and spinach, but can be served with long pasta as well.

Serves 4–6

2 cups walnuts

1 roll of bread, crust removed

½ cup whole milk

½ cup pine nuts

1 clove garlic

1 teaspoon marjoram leaves, finely chopped

1 teaspoon of salt

½ cup olive oil

¼ cup grated Parmigiano, plus some for serving

1 pound fettuccine (or other long pasta, or ravioli)

Bring a large pot of salted water to a boil. Add the walnuts and cook for 5 minutes. Remove the nuts, let them cool, pat dry, and rub them in a cotton towel in order to remove as much of their skin as possible.

Soak the bread in milk. When soggy, squeeze the milk back into the bowl where it was soaked. Set the bread and milk aside.

Place the walnuts in a food processor (or use a mortar and pestle), along with the pine nuts, garlic, marjoram and bread, with some salt. Blend together until a thick paste is formed. Add some of the retained milk until a thick, creamy consistency is achieved. Add more salt to taste. Remove the mixture to a bowl, and drizzle in the olive oil, and then mix in the Parmigiano. Add more of the retained milk if necessary to achieve a creamy consistency.

Bring another large pot of salted water to a boil.

Cook the pasta until *al dente* (about 2 minutes less than the package directions), drain, and reserve 1 cup of the cooking water. Place the pasta in a serving bowl and slowly mix in the nut sauce. Add a bit of the reserved cooking water if it seems too dry.

Sprinkle with Parmigiano and serve immediately.

VINO

Bianco: Pigato or Vermentino

Rosso: Dolcetto

Liguria's fresh reds and whites pair best with this pasta. Pigato and Vermentino are the region's signature white grapes. While the few existing examples of profound and concentrated Pigato might work here, Vermentino is the ticket. Medium to full-body versions of Vermentino are scented with walnuts and lemon zest. Liguria's best indigenous reds are Ormeasco, as Dolcetto is locally known, and Rossese. These reds offer a generous fruitiness to lift this decadent pasta.

LASAGNA AI FUNGHI E TARTUFI
Lasagna with Mushrooms and Truffles

Benedict is the first Pope to retire in nearly 600 years, proof that the Vatican must be a really exciting place to live. Still, if I were a priest, I think I would prefer to live in The Big Easy, The City That Care Forgot—in New Orleans, where the confessionals probably are enough to make a reality TV producer blush. Still, as mischievous as the city can be, some folks are more pious, asking for little more than a winning Saints game and good bowl of pasta on Sundays.

As proof that our prayers are answered, this recipe is provided by Monsignor Christopher Nalty, who recently returned to New Orleans after ten years at the Vatican. In Rome, he became a devout believer in pasta, and is said to have kept his fellow priests well-fed with an inspired *bucatini all'amatriciana*. Back in New Orleans, he is still nourishing his flock, and recently prepared this *lasagna ai funghi e tartufi* (which he adapted from Taverna Giula in Rome). Sinful maybe, but this lasagna is truly heaven-sent.

Serves 6–8

- 1 ½ pounds mushrooms—any mixture of fresh or 6 ounces dried porcini
- ¼ cup olive oil, plus some for the baking dish
- Salt to taste
- Freshly ground white pepper to taste
- 3 ounces truffle oil
- 3 cups Béchamel sauce (recipe below)
- 16 ounces mozzarella, chopped
- 1 pound lasagna, preferably fresh, thin sheets, egg pasta, parboiled
- Grated Parmigiano

Heat the oven to 350°F. This lasagna will be about seven thin layers, so use a deep baking dish.

Wash the mushrooms thoroughly in cold water. If using dried porcini, reconstitute them in water according to the package directions. Slice the fresh mushrooms into bite-sized pieces. In a large skillet, over medium heat, sauté the mushrooms in ¼ cup olive oil. Cover and simmer 10–15 minutes until their liquid evaporates and they are well cooked. Add salt and pepper to taste. Drizzle with half of the truffle oil, and remove from heat.

Assemble the Lasagna:

Drizzle the bottom of the baking dish with olive oil, and then add the first sheet of pasta. Cover with a kitchen spoonful of béchamel, then some mushrooms, then some mozzarella. Add another layer of pasta, and repeat the layers, using a proportionate amount of béchamel, mushrooms and mozzarella between the pasta layers. Sprinkle the top layer with grated Parmigiano, and cover with foil, and bake for 30 minutes. Remove the foil and broil until the top is golden brown and the sides are bubbling. Let rest for ten minutes. Serve, topped with shaved truffles.

Béchamel Sauce

- ½ cup flour
- 8 ounces butter
- 3 cups whole milk
- 1 teaspoon nutmeg
- Salt to taste
- Freshly ground white pepper to taste
- 1 ounce black truffle, shaved or minced*

In a non-reactive saucepan over medium heat, melt the butter and stir in the flour. Cook, stirring continuously with a wooden spoon, for 3 minutes. Add the milk. Add the nutmeg, salt, and pepper. Mix in half the truffles and the remaining truffle oil. Stir until the mixture is slightly thicker than buttermilk.

*If not available, porcini or other mushrooms are possible substitutes.

VINO
Bianco: Falanghina
Rosso: Aglianico

Mushrooms and truffles share aromas of forest floor and fallen leaves, and they beg for wines with smoky minerality. Both whites from Campania and reds from Basilicata, typically grown in volcanic soils that give the wines a smoky character, make excellent matches. Falanghina tends to be citrusy and somewhat neutral. The Aglianico reds of Basilicata carry a similar smoky savoriness and are more mineral than fruit-driven, perfect for this lasagna.

MANICOTTI CON SALSA DI POMODORO
Manicotti with Tomato Sauce

Christmas Eve for me just wouldn't be complete without a hearty serving of manicotti and a teary viewing of "It's a Wonderful Life." I love Capra's mushy masterpiece and can now proudly recite large portions of it by heart. Still, there are a few things about it that really bother me. 1) I hate that song "Buffalo Gals." 2) I know it's about the season of peace and joy, but I would like to punch that Mr. Potter right in the schnoz, and that moron Uncle Billy too. And while I'm at it, that ingrate brother Harry who took his sweet time coming home. And 3), there's that whole scene when George sees what Bedford Falls would be like if he had never existed. I simply don't buy it.

Alas, as irritating as it is, I will watch and weep again this year and remember that no matter how tough life gets, "No man is a failure who has friends," which makes me "the richest man in town." Fade to *Auld Lang Syne* … Hugs to wifey and Zuzu. A bell rings, and an angel gets its wings.

Serves 4–6, makes about 12 manicotti

- 1 medium onion, finely chopped
- ½ cup olive oil
- 1 28 ounce can plum tomatoes, puréed
- 1 teaspoon salt
- ½ teaspoon freshly ground black pepper
- 4–5 basil leaves, chopped
- 1 cup all-purpose flour
- 1 cup whole milk
- ⅓ cup water
- 2 large eggs
- 1 pound whole milk ricotta cheese
- 2 tablespoons grated Parmigiano plus more for serving
- ⅓ cup chopped flat-leaf parsley
- 1 teaspoon salt

In a large skillet over medium heat, sauté the onion in the olive oil until golden. Add the tomatoes, salt, pepper and basil. Reduce heat and simmer for about 20–30 minutes, until the sauce has reduced.

In a large bowl, whisk together the flour, milk, water and 1 egg until smooth.

Place a large skillet or griddle over low heat. Use butter to grease the surface. Pour ⅛ cup batter onto the hot surface. Let the batter to cook through, but not turn golden. Use a spatula to remove and set aside. Re-grease the surface and repeat until all the batter is used. Ideally, the mixture will yield 12 sheets of pasta, 3 × 5 or 4 × 6 inches wide. (Note: if using a skillet, they can be round in shape.)

In a large bowl, add the ricotta, Parmigiano cheese, remaining egg, parsley and salt. Mix together until creamy.

Carefully fill the center of each pasta sheet with 2 heaping tablespoons of the ricotta mixture. Fold one side over the other to make to enclose. Line them up in an oiled baking dish. Cover loosely with foil and bake at 350°F. for 30 minutes, until the sides are bubbling.

Serve immediately with a spoonful of tomato sauce and grated Parmigiano.

VINO

Bianco: Tubiana, a.k.a. Trebbiano di Lugana
Rosso: Barbera d'Asti

Manicotti needs wines with mouthwatering acidity to cut through the ricotta. While palate relief is necessary, the tannins from red wines should be conservative. Trebbiano di Lugana shows flavors of yellow plum and white peaches, which meld nicely with the tomatoes and herbal parsley notes. Barbera has red cherry and plum flavors that offer youthful fruit to match this dish's generous and fruit-driven mid-palate.

RIGATONI CON LE POLPETTINE
Rigatoni with Meatballs

Oh, if I could only hold my dear grandmother's hand just one more time… I would make a mold of it, of her palm—the very palm that produced the most perfect-sized meatballs ever made. Of course, questions about secret ingredients and how much pressure she exerted would remain unanswered, but at least one variable would be removed from my quest to replicate the world's best meatball. Below is all the information we have available. She got the recipe from her mother-in-law from Avellino, in Campania.

Like so many Italian foods in America, especially the ones with southern Italian origins, there is a misconception that meatballs are somehow more American than Italian. We can argue about the correct pasta pairing, the appropriate size of the ball, at what point they should be eaten during the meal, and even about the different potential ingredients, but there is no doubt that a meatball, correctly prepared, is very Italian, albeit southern Italian. There is certainly no doubt that it is universally loved. So please, practice away, teach your kids, and pass down your own little ball of happiness.

Note: My grandmother claimed that the order in which the ingredients are combined is key. And also, you need some patience: fry them slowly over low heat.

Serves 4–6

For the sauce, see recipe on page 30

For the meatballs:

1 teaspoon salt
½ teaspoon freshly ground white pepper
2 tablespoons grated Parmigiano or Pecorino Romano
¼ cup finely chopped flat-leaf parsley
2 cloves garlic, finely chopped
2 eggs, beaten
4 slices Italian bread, crusts removed
Milk, as needed—water as an alternative
1 pound chopped beef, preferably sirloin
Olive oil for frying
1 pound rigatoni—or any pasta
Grated Parmigiano to serve

For the meatballs:

In a large bowl, mix together the salt, pepper, Parmigiano, parsley, and garlic. Add the beaten eggs and mix. Dip the bread in milk or water, squeeze out most of the liquid and mix it into the egg mixture. When the ingredients are thoroughly combined, add the meat and use your hands to combine. If the mixture seems dry, add a tablespoon or two of water. Take a handful of the meat mixture, shape into a medium sized ball—about 2 ounces, maximum, and repeat until you have used all of the meat mixture. In a large skillet, over medium-low heat, add ¼ cup of olive oil. When the oil is hot, place the meatballs in the skillet, with enough room to allow you to easily flip them over. Cook the meatballs, in batches, until brown on all sides—careful not to burn them. Remove them from the skillet and add to the tomato sauce, and cook together, over low heat, for about an hour.

Bring a large pot of salted water to a boil.

Cook the pasta until *al dente* (about 2 minutes less than the package directions). Drain and place in a serving bowl. Mix in some sauce.

Serve with two meatballs per person and grated Parmigiano.

VINO

Rosso: Gaglioppo and Nero di Troia

Wines rich in fruit, full in body and moderate in acidity, especially from Southern Italy, will match the weight of this dish. The Italian grapes Gaglioppo and Nero di Troia make wines with substantial fruit and full body, and their mildly tugging tannins will keep the pasta focused on the palate. Gaglioppo shows distinctive floral notes and Nero di Troia offers aromas of lavender and anise.

WINTER
RECIPES

CAVATELLI CON RAGÙ ALLA NAPOLETANA

Cavatelli with Gravy and Braciola

You know what they say: no talk of sex, politics, religion, or *ragù* at the dinner table. Of all these taboo dinner topics, the most incendiary and divisive for Italians may be how to prepare a proper *ragù* (also known as "gravy" to many Italian Americans, although even that name is controversial).

No pasta meal brings back more memories for me than that of *rigatoni* or *cavatelli* with a hearty gravy at my grandparents' house on Sunday afternoons. All of that chaos and delight, the yelling, laughing, hiding, and eating way too much food, inspired me to create *Sunday Pasta*.

All *ragù* is local. It is a personal thing, a family thing. And so is *braciola*. Here is my grandmother's recipe for "gravy with braciole." Every Italian family from the area around Naples has its own recipe for this dish, but it just so happens that my grandmother's is the best! Like I said, it's best to avoid controversial topics around dinner. I don't mean to stir things up, but some topics are too important to ignore.

Serves 4–6

- 4 slices of beef, preferably rump steak (about 6 ounces each, sliced or pounded thin, to about ¼")
- 4 slices bacon or pancetta
- 4 slices salame (Genoa or other Italian variety)
- 2 eggs
- 4 ounces Pecorino, Parmigiano or provolone cheese, grated or cut in small pieces
- ¼ cup Italian flat leaf parsley, coarsely chopped
- 2 cloves garlic, finely chopped
- 1 cup white wine
- 2 28-ounce cans Italian peeled tomatoes, puréed
- ¼ cup breadcrumbs
- Salt, to taste
- Freshly ground pepper, to taste
- ¼ cup olive oil
- 1 pound cavatelli (or rigatoni)

Boil the eggs until hard. Let cool, cut into small pieces, set aside. Finely chop the salame, garlic, and parsley and mix together.

Pat dry the beef slices. Lightly salt and pepper the top side of each. Line them up on a work surface. Place a slice of bacon on the center of each. Evenly spread the salame mixture on top of the bacon, evenly distribute the egg and cheese. Sprinkle with breadcrumbs.

Starting with the narrower end (of the beef), carefully roll up each slice, tightly, and fasten with tooth picks.

Heat the olive oil in a large pan over medium heat. Add the braciole, carefully turning until each side is lightly brown. Add the wine and cook for a few minutes, then add the tomatoes, and salt and pepper to taste. Reduce the heat to low and cook for about 2 hours, stirring, frequently and carefully.

Bring a large pot of salted water to a boil.

Cook the pasta until *al dente* (about 2 minutes less than the package directions), drain, and add to a serving bowl, lightly coat with ragu. Serve immediately with additional sauce and a sprinkle of Parmigiano. Serve the braciole on a separate platter.

VINO

Rosso: Morellino di Scansano

Morellino di Scansano is based on the noble Sangiovese grape and comes from a warmer, flatter stretch near Tuscany's coast, resulting in a Sangiovese with richer, darker flavors: black rather than red cherries, moderate versus perky acidity, rounder versus sharper tannins. Morellino is a more succulent Sangiovese wine, just like all the wonderfully fatty meats in this pasta.

TAGLIATELLE AI FUNGHI PORCINI
Tagliatelle with Porcini Mushrooms

This little porcini went to market. This little porcini stayed home. And this little porcini went wee, wee, wee, all the way onto my tagliatelle. Porcini mushrooms, from the plural for *porcino*, or piglet, are a favorite of man and swine alike. Formally known as *boletus edulis*, it is said they have been given the name porcini over the centuries in Italy both because they look like piglets and because pigs love to eat them.

Boldly flavored Porcini are very versatile, partially because they can be dried, and then reconstituted with water, but also because they're delicious with pasta, risotto, soup, and even on their own, as a *contorno* (side dish). Although Italian folklore has it that they sprout with the new moon, in reality they do well with a lot of summer rain, followed by the autumn drop in soil temperature. You and your piggies can find porcini near pine, spruce, hemlock and fir trees, but I suggest that you pay a little more and get them at the market and therefore more quickly onto your own tagliatelle.

Serves 4–6

1 pound porcini mushrooms, or 8 ounces if using dried
2 cloves garlic, finely chopped
¼ cup olive oil
Salt to taste
¼ cup flat-leaf parsley, coarsely chopped
Freshly ground black pepper to taste
1 pound tagliatelle, or fettuccine
Grated Parmigiano

Clean the mushrooms. If using dried porcini, soak them in cold water for 20–30 minutes until their size and moisture are restored. Slice them into bite-sized pieces.

In a large skillet, over medium heat sauté the garlic in the olive oil until it's golden. Add the mushrooms and cook over medium heat for 15–20 minutes. Add salt and pepper to taste.

Bring a large pot of salted water to a boil.

Cook the pasta until *al dente* (about 2 minutes less than the package directions). Drain, and retain one cup of the cooking water. Add the pasta to the mushrooms. Add the parsley, and then cook together for about a minute. Add some of the retained cooking water if the pasta seems too dry.

Serve with grated Parmigiano.

VINO
Bianco: Chardonnay
Rosso: Pinot Nero

Mushrooms of all types work particularly well with wines made from grapes in the Pinot family. Cool climate Chardonnay smells of fresh apples when young, but as the wine reaches five to six years of age, it begins to smell of earth and straw. It is best to choose a wine from Italy's northern, cooler regions. Pinot Nero smells like a walk in the woods in autumn, tying into the mushroom's aromas. Its tannins are soft but its acidity is invigorating, and palate cleansing.

STRANGOZZI CON LE CAPESANTE
Strangozzi with Scallops

It happened one day. On a cold, gray Saturday in January. The journey, from Slovenia to Venice, driven by the thought of lunch on the Grand Canal. The rest is a dreamlike blur … See sign for the Italian border. Forget Venice, too far away. Take first exit, Trieste. Happen upon *Menarosti, Antico Ristorante dal 1903*. Enter an unassuming doorway to find tables full of Italians eating, talking, and laughing. In the back room, nonna, shelling crabs by hand. Mother and daughter, keeping watch over the dining room, with son in the kitchen. After a brief conversation about all that came in from the lagoon that morning, eight delicious courses: various fish, shrimp, clams, scallops. Fried, raw, baked, with pasta. And local Friulano wine. A thought occurs: karma. There will surely be payback for my good fortune. But that worry will keep for another day. Or at least, until after espresso.

My friends at *Menarosti* have been kind enough to send me their recipe, which I adapted below. I doubt you can get your scallops fresh from the Istrian lagoon, and I doubt your *strangozzi* will come from Umbria, but this will get you close enough to share the dream. You can deal with karma later.

Serves 4–6

- 1 shallot, finely chopped
- 2 tablespoons olive oil
- ½ cup white wine
- 1 pound cherry tomatoes, rinsed, stems removed, cut into wedges
- 2 sprigs thyme
- Salt to taste
- Freshly ground black pepper to taste
- 12 sea scallops, cleaned
- 16 ounces fish stock
- ¼ cup brandy
- 1 pound strangozzi, tagliatelle or linguine
- 2 tablespoons chopped flat-leaf parsley

In a large skillet over medium heat sauté the shallots in 1 tablespoon olive oil until translucent. Add the wine, tomatoes, 1 thyme sprig, salt and pepper to taste.

In another pan over medium heat, quickly brown the scallops in 1 tablespoon olive oil with the remaining thyme sprig. Add the brandy.

Bring a large pot of salted water to a boil.

Add the fish stock to the tomatoes and cook on high heat for 10 minutes. Taste for salt and pepper and add as desired.

Cook the strangozzi until *al dente* (about 2 minutes less than the package directions), drain and add to the tomato sauce. Add the scallops. Toss with the parsley.

Serve immediately.

VINO
Frizzante: Prosecco
Bianco: Friulano Blends

Scallops, cherry tomatoes, brandy and white wine share a common element: light sweetness. Prosecco is one of the best vinous complements to the succulent scallop, as it is typically made in a sweeter style. (Counterintuitively, for sweeter styles, look for "Extra Dry" and "Dry" on the label. "Brut" indicates the drier styles.) Prosecco's delicate floral fragrance conjures up gardens of wisteria and acacia—pairing well with the dish's thyme, parsley and tomatoes.

LASAGNA ALLA BOLOGNESE
Lasagna with Meat Sauce

We know you're in there, Mr. Chips. Step away from your vehicle, Senor Guacamole. Come out with your hands up, Mr. Wings. We don't want anyone to get hurt. It's Super Bowl Sunday and there's a new sheriff in town. His name is Lasagna Bolognese and he's riding a blazing saddle. He's packing major heat, too. For sure, he'll outlaw loitering around the seven layer dip. Forget about that time bomb, chili con carne; it only disturbs the peace.

For all of us seeking to maintain law and order this Sunday, Sheriff Bolognese is guaranteed to keep the hooligans at bay. So, whether you're on the field, out tailgating, or at home, this Bolognese will save the day.

Serves 6–8

1 onion, coarsely chopped
1 carrot, peeled, finely chopped
1 celery stalk, finely chopped
1 bay leaf
¼ cup olive oil
¾ pound ground beef—20% fat is best
¼ pound ground pork
3 slices prosciutto finely chopped
1 6-ounce can tomato paste
¼ cup dry white wine
1 35-ounce can plum tomatoes, puréed
2 eggs
1 pound whole milk ricotta cheese
½ cup grated Parmigiano, plus more for garnish
1 teaspoon salt
1 teaspoon freshly ground black pepper
1 pound mozzarella cheese, diced
1 pound lasagna sheets

In a large, heavy-bottom pot over medium heat sauté the onion, celery, carrot and bay leaf in the olive oil until onion is translucent. Add ground beef, pork, and prosciutto to the sautéed vegetables, and use a wooden spoon to break up the meat and combine with the vegetables. When the meat is nearly cooked, add tomato paste and stir to fully incorporate. Add white wine and simmer until the wine evaporates. Add the crushed tomatoes and ½ can (from the tomatoes) water.

Bring the sauce to a boil and then reduce to a simmer. Cook, uncovered, for approximately 2 hours until reduced. Add salt and pepper to taste.

Bring a large pot of salted water to a boil.

In a large bowl, mix eggs into the ricotta. Add the Parmigiano, ½ teaspoon each of salt and pepper, and ¾ of the mozzarella.

Cook the lasagna sheets for half of the manufacturer's suggested cooking time, drain and set aside. Coat the bottom of a baking pan—9 × 11 or other similar size at least 3″ deep—with a little olive oil, and then cover with ¾ cup of sauce. Place a layer of lasagna, a layer of the ricotta mixture and ¾ cup of sauce. Repeat layers until you reach the top of the pan. Depending on the depth and size of the pan, you may have leftover lasagna, or you can make more layers with slightly less filling between layers. Cover top with a layer of lasagna and ¾ cup of the sauce, the remaining mozzarella and a generous amount of grated Parmigiano. Cover with aluminum foil and cook at 350° F for about 30 minutes. Remove foil and cook for another 10–15 minutes until top is browned and the sides are bubbling.

Remove from oven and let rest for 10 minutes before serving.

VINO
Bianco: Nosiola
Rosso: Teroldego

This dish begs for red wine with enough chewy tannin and cleansing acidity to cut through its density. However, the vegetables and bay leaf give an aromatic intensity that opens a window to white wine. Nosiola from Trentino is moderately fragrant white with notes of hay and hazelnuts that match well with this pasta. Full-flavored with smoke, spice and blackberries, Teroldego, also from Trentino, makes rather robust wines which pair well with hearty, meat-heavy dishes.

PENNONE CON CAVOLFIORE AL FORNO

Baked Pennone with Cauliflower

I am strongly opposed to eating genetically modified foods. No GMOs for my loved ones! I am willing to make an exception, however, and that is for cauliflower. I can only hope that Monsanto alters the heck out of it. Maybe they can give it some color, so it looks less like a human brain. And then perhaps they can add a pleasant flavor. And oh, that smell.

On the other hand, our cruciferous friend is chock full of vitamins and nutrients. It is high in dietary fiber, folate, water, and vitamin C. It also contains many phytochemicals that may protect against cancer. (Boiling it reduces the potency of many of these compounds, which is why I recommend steaming, roasting, or lightly frying it.)

OK, upon further reflection, maybe it's better to save cauliflower from Monsanto, along with the rest of our foods. Don't get me wrong. I'm still not a huge fan of cauliflower, but luckily, we have plenty of cheese and pancetta to make it delicious for everyone. And for those who naturally love it, you'll love it even more as prepared below.

Serves: 4–6

- 1 ½ pounds of cauliflower, cut into florets
- ¼ cup olive oil
- 2 cloves garlic
- 6 ounces pancetta, cut into small cubes (optional)
- 4 ounces scamorza, provolone, or fontina cheese, cut into small pieces
- ¾ cup heavy cream (optional)
- 4 ounces Parmigiano cheese, grated
- 4 ounces breadcrumbs
- 2 ounces butter
- Salt, to taste
- Pepper, to taste
- Crushed red pepper
- 1 pound rigatoni or other tubular pasta

In a large skillet, sauté the garlic in the olive oil until golden. Remove the garlic. If using pancetta, add it and sauté until light golden. Add the cauliflower and then enough water to almost cover it. Cook, covered for 5–10 minutes, then uncovered for another 5 minutes until water is mostly evaporated. The cauliflower should be tender, but not mushy. Add about 1 teaspoon each of salt, black pepper and/or crushed red pepper, depending on your taste.

Bring a large pot of salted water to a boil.

Cook the pasta until very *al dente* (about 3–4 minutes less than the package's instructions) and drain it. Place the pasta into an oven-proof casserole. Mix in the cauliflower, add the cream if you are using it, and then sprinkle the cheese and breadcrumbs evenly across the top. Add a few small pats of butter. Place under the broiler for 5–10 minutes until the cheese is melted and golden brown. Serve immediately.

VINO

Bianco: Friulano Chardonnay

Rosso: Friulano Merlot and Cabernet Sauvignon Blends

The robust flavors of this dish make it one of those rare pastas that can take a little new oak in stride. With all the creamy goodness here, why not pick up a rich Chardonnay or a Chardonnay-blend from Friuli? And why not stick with "international" grapes for the reds, too? In Friuli, there are some beautiful Merlot and Cabernet Sauvignon blends that have just enough fruitiness to contrast the earthiness of the cauliflower.

TIMPANO PANTHEON

Meat and Pasta Pie

Perhaps the most noble profession of all is that of the architect, whose calling is to leave the world useful gifts of lasting beauty; pieces of his heart and mind that inspire us in turn. Although we live in a time when architecture in New York faces death by committee and even Rome questions whether it can afford to save ancient masterpieces, what we gain from a beautiful building pays society back in spades. What value can be placed on the energy that emanates from the Pantheon or the Empire State Building?

I've often wondered whether the food in Rome is as miraculous as I believe it to be, or whether, just maybe, it tastes better because I'm so intoxicated by the city's architecture. For me, it's impossible to separate the two sensory experiences.

A *timpano*—a.k.a. *timballo*—is pasta baked within a pastry shell or mold. Coincidentally, it's also the Italian architectural term for tympanum, e.g., the triangular space above the columns in the Pantheon. A timpano can take the shape of whatever baking dish it is prepared in, but I rather prefer it in the shape of a dome, like the one atop the Pantheon.

Almost all regions of Italy have their own version. The dish, of course, was made famous by the 1996 movie *Big Night*.

Serves 6

- 1 onion, coarsely chopped
- ½ cup olive oil
- 1 pound sweet Italian sausage, casings removed, crumbled
- 1 cup white wine
- 1 35-ounce can peeled plum tomatoes, puréed
- 1 teaspoon salt
- 1 teaspoon freshly ground black pepper
- 2 eggs
- 1 cup heavy cream
- ½ cup grated Parmigiano
- ¼ cup unseasoned breadcrumbs
- 1 pound pappardelle or tagliatelle
- 10 ounces green peas—thawed, if frozen
- Butter for the baking dish

In a large skillet over medium heat, sauté the onion in the olive oil until lightly golden. Add the sausage and cook until no pink remains in the meat. Add the wine and let it evaporate. Add the tomatoes, salt and pepper. Lower the heat and cook for about 30 minutes, or until reduced.

While the tomato sauce is cooking, beat the eggs in a mixing bowl and mix in the cream and Parmigiano. Set aside.

Bring a large pot of salted water to boil.

Butter the inside of a large baking dish or cake pan, at least 2 quart capacity—shape is not important. Add the breadcrumbs and tilt the pan from side to side until they are evenly distributed.

Cook the pasta for half of the manufacturer's instructions and drain. Place the pasta in a large mixing bowl and add in the tomato sauce. Line the bottom of the baking dish with a single layer of the pappardelle coated in tomato sauce.

Heat the oven to 350°F.

Add the peas, and cream mixture into the remaining pasta and mix together. Then add the pasta mixture into the baking dish. Bake about an hour or until golden brown and the sides are bubbling.

Let settle for about 10 minutes and then flip onto a serving platter, cut into wedges and serve.

VINO

Bianco: Pigato

Rosso: Granaccia

The key to a good pairing here is rip-roaring acidity. The wine also needs good fruit juiciness and medium to medium-plus body to match the dish. Pigato, known as Vermentino in Tuscany and Sardinia, offers citrus and floral aromas that work with the green peas and tomatoes. Granaccia, akin to the Cannonau of Sardinia and the Grenache of Southern Rhône, possesses a vibrant red fruit and spice complex that integrates with the dish's many components.

SPAGHETTI ALLA CARBONARA

Spaghetti with Pancetta and Eggs

Sometimes it's easier to have just a few choices rather than too many. This notion is so simple, and perhaps a bit bourgeois. But the intersection of freedom and rules can be tricky, especially in the kitchen, where you literally eat your bad judgment. Along these lines, take spaghetti *alla carbonara,* a simple mixture of bacon, egg, spaghetti, and cheese that is so often over thought and overwrought.

I'm going to be specific here, but give you some wiggle room within the constraints. (This, even though a chef in Rome recently told me that the only correct way to prepare the dish is per the recipe provided below.) Your first choice is between pancetta (pork belly) and guanciale (pork jowl). Guanciale has a more intense flavor, but is fattier. Next, choose between whole eggs or just the yolks. Last, for cheese, will you go with the sharper Pecorino Romano (correct) or Parmigiano-Reggiano (acceptable)? Within these boundaries, just play around with the ingredients and quantities you like. The only sin you can commit is to add cream (as most all Italian-American restaurants do). So experiment away. Go crazy. And if you wish to stray altogether feel free. Just don't call it *carbonara*.

Serves 4–6

- 2 whole eggs, beaten
- 2 egg yolks, beaten
- ½ cup grated Pecorino Romano cheese, plus more for serving
- 6 ounces guanciale or pancetta
- Freshly ground black pepper
- 1 pound spaghetti

Cut the pancetta into ½ inch strips or cubes.

In a bowl, combine the beaten eggs, yolks, and grated Pecorino. Set aside.

Bring a large pot of salted water to a boil.

In a large skillet over medium heat, cook the pancetta until golden—careful not to overcook it. Remove the skillet from heat.*

Cook the pasta until *al dente* (about 2 minutes less than the package directions), drain and add it to the guanciale. When thoroughly combined, quickly add the egg and cheese mixture. Serve immediately, with a few grinds of black pepper and some grated Pecorino Romano cheese.

Note: In Rome, guanciale is often favored, but I prefer the meatier pancetta. Carbonara can be tricky. The result should be creamy. If the skillet is too hot when you add the eggs, they may scramble. Try it until you get it right!

VINO

Bianco: Central Italian "Orange" Wine Blends
Rosso: Umbrian Blends

Spaghetti Carbonara tastes rich but feels light. Its wine pairing should be medium-bodied with some mouth-coating glycerol to match this dish's richness. The wine should also show enough acidic nerve to cleanse the palate. Finally, its fruit should be fairly restrained. Wines from Central Italy, especially blends, offer easy-drinking, combining a simplicity and brightness of crowd-pleasing fruit that contrasts with the pasta's profound flavors.

PASTA E FAGIOLI
Pasta and Beans

On this Valentine's Day, I reflect back to when I first met Patricia, the ideal modern woman, desirable on so many levels: artistic, strong, beautiful, and smart. I placed her high upon a pedestal. And being the saint that I am, I did this despite the fact that her cooking skills left something to be desired. Judge not, I thought, she is a victim of the times—times during which it was simply not fashionable to "just stay home to bake cookies." But she loves good food and is a quick study. And so, after many culinary renditions of "The Rain in Spain," I am most pleased to debut Patricia's version of *Pasta e Fagioli*. You've come a long way, baby! And I must say, as an ideal modern man, I am ecstatic that American society now recognizes that the art of cooking transcends both gender and politics. Cooking is giving and giving is love. And love is universal. So cook your heart out. Spread your love with food. And do it with Patricia's *Pasta e Fagioli*!

Serves 4–6

- 1 onion, finely chopped
- 1 celery stalk, finely chopped
- 1 carrot, peeled and finely chopped
- 2 cloves garlic, finely chopped
- ¼ cup olive oil
- 6 basil leaves
- 4 ounces pancetta, diced
- 2 16 ounce cans cooked cannellini beans
- 1 bay leaf
- ¾ pound ditalini or other short tubular pasta
- Grated Parmigiano for serving
- 1 teaspoon salt to taste
- 1 teaspoon freshly ground black pepper to taste

In a large pot, over medium heat, sauté the onions, celery, carrot, and garlic in the olive oil until the onion is translucent. Add the basil. In a separate skillet, cook the pancetta until golden brown. Add the pancetta to the vegetables, lower the heat and cook for 2–3 minutes.

Place ⅓ of the beans in a small bowl and mash them with a fork until they become a paste. Add the remaining beans and the bean paste to the vegetable mixture. Add the salt and pepper, then mix the ingredients for another minute over low heat. Add 4–6 cups of water, to cover the beans. Add the bay leaf. Raise the heat to boil the liquid. Add the pasta. Cook the pasta *al dente* (about 2 minutes less than package directions). Add additional water if there is insufficient liquid. [Depending on your preference,] the result should be a thick soup.

Serve with salt and pepper to taste and grated Parmigiano.

Note: Like so many popular Italian dishes, there are multiple versions of *Pasta e Fagioli*—not just one for each region, but more like one for each town, or one for each kitchen. You can use any type of beans, broth instead of water, add tomatoes, prosciutto, and any variety of spices (like bay leaf, parsley, sage, thyme, basil, etc.,) and instead of short pasta, you can simply break long pasta into pieces. It's all pasta e fagioli!

VINO
Spumante: Franciacorta
Bianco: Pignoletto

This hearty soup needs dry and crisp wines to counter it with refreshment. Though a soft red like a Pinot Nero from the north can work, whites and sparklers are ideal from a flavor perspective. Crisp sparkling wines from Franciacorta are produced in the *methodo classico*, the same way Champagne is made. For a still white, a mouthwatering option try the unsung Pignoletto, which clings to Bologna's hills and is a regional specialty.

SPAGHETTI ALLA PUTTANESCA
Spaghetti with Olives, Capers, and Anchovies

This is a difficult subject to broach in any context, but particularly so in a prim and proper family book such as this, where it would be absolutely gauche to mention Dominique Strauss-Kahn, Elliot Spitzer, or their libertine friends. But if you-know-what is the world's oldest profession, then *spaghetti puttanesca* must be the world's oldest pasta recipe. And there is no shame in that. In fact, those working girls who created it really did know a little something about spicy, cheap, and easy. A touch of this, a handful of that, with a little bite, and a big kick, this dish delivers every time. No questions asked. Satisfaction guaranteed.

So judge not, lest ye be judged! In my humble opinion, *spaghetti puttanesca* makes up for at least a few of their sins. Now invite your friends and enjoy! (But please don't use taxpayers' money.)

Serves 4–6

- 3 cloves garlic, finely chopped
- 6 anchovy fillets, finely chopped
- ½ cup olive oil
- ½ cup black olives, pitted and chopped
- 1 28-ounce can peeled plum tomatoes, drained and chopped—or 6 tomatoes peeled and seeded
- 2 tablespoons capers
- 1 tablespoon chopped flat-leaf parsley
- 1 pound spaghetti

Bring a large pot of salted water to a boil.

In a large skillet over medium heat sauté the garlic and anchovies in the olive oil until garlic is golden. Add the tomatoes, olives and capers. Cook on medium heat for 15–20 minutes, until reduced.

Cook the spaghetti until *al dente* (about 2 minutes less than the package directions) and drain it. Add to the tomato sauce and mix to thoroughly combine.

Serve immediately garnished with parsley.

VINO
Bianco: Grecante or Falanghina
Rosso: Primitivo or Aglianico

This assertive pasta demands very specific wines, such as Central and southern Italian whites that have the medium body and broad mid-palate to support the boldness of the dish. They also show heartier, more savory elements as opposed to the lighter herbal notes typical in northern Italian whites. The capers and tomatoes in this pasta contribute brightness, so a wine with red berry lift will meld better than one whose flavors are focused exclusively on black fruits.

ZITI AL FORNO

Baked Ziti

Pasta al forno, or baked pasta (ziti in this case), is a triple comfort food. First, although almost any type of pasta can be used, the very thought of "baked ziti" is sure to bring back warm memories from years ago, when it was a staple at school functions and family gatherings. Then there is the physical comfort that comes when you taste the hot, oozing mixture of cheese and sauce, especially on a cold day. And finally, there is the heartfelt praise you receive for serving it. My own kids sprang from their chairs to hug me when they tasted it. So if you make it, you'll be in for an Italian comfort food trifecta. You'll be thrice warmed. But some words of caution: although I am certain about the nostalgic impact and the delicious recipe, whether you actually earn the hugs will depend on *your own* culinary skills and *your* personality. Unfortunately, these things are beyond my control.

Serves 8

- 2 onions, finely chopped
- ½ cup olive oil
- 2 28-ounce cans peeled plum tomatoes, puréed
- 8–12 basil leaves
- 2 teaspoons salt
- 1 ½ teaspoons freshly ground black pepper
- 1 pound whole milk ricotta
- 2 eggs
- 2 tablespoons chopped flat-leaf parsley
- 3 tablespoons grated Parmigiano, plus extra for serving
- ½ pound mozzarella, diced
- 1 pound ziti or other tubular pasta
- 1 teaspoon freshly ground pepper

In a large skillet over medium heat, sauté the onions until they're golden brown. Add the tomatoes to the onion. Add the basil, one teaspoon salt, and one-half teaspoon pepper. Reduce the heat and simmer, uncovered for 1 hour or until reduced.

Bring a large pot of salted water to a boil.

In a large bowl combine the ricotta, eggs, parsley, 2 tablespoons Parmigiano, ¾ of the diced mozzarella and the remaining salt and pepper.

Cook the pasta for half of the manufacturer's directions. Drain, and add it to the ricotta mixture. Mix in half of the tomato sauce. Coat the bottom of a 9 × 12 inch baking pan with a spoonful of sauce. Add the pasta mixture to the pan. Cover with the remaining mozzarella and Parmigiano and a few spoonfuls of tomato sauce. Bake, uncovered, at 350°F for approximately 30 minutes or until the top is golden brown and the sides are bubbling.

Serve immediately with a spoonful of sauce and grated Parmigiano.

VINO

Bianco: Trebbiano d'Abruzzo
Rosso: Montepulciano d'Abruzzo

Comfort food welcomes comfort wines. Abruzzo's medium-bodied, moderate acidity, sunshine-driven quaffers are highly reliable and mostly very inexpensive. Two varieties dominate Abruzzese wines, most of which are varietal: Trebbiano in white and Montepulciano in red. Trebbiano has a plush palate to match the pasta's weight. Montepulciano's red plum and cherry flavors mesh with the tomato sauce both in terms of flavor and juiciness on the palate.

SPAGHETTI CON BOTTARGA
Spaghetti with Fish Roe

If your idea of intellectual stimulation is watching a Britney Spears interview, then read no further. If, however, you are interested in the happy confluence that is my favorite book, Italian restaurant, and pasta dish, then you've come to the right place.

Il Gattopardo, one of my favorite Italian restaurants in NYC, is the namesake of my favorite book, *Il Gattopardo (The Leopard)* written by Giuseppe Tomasi di Lampedusa, published in 1958, a year after his death. (Luchino Visconti made the movie in 1963, but I don't think it does the book justice.) It's the story of the Prince of Salina, during the waning days of Sicilian aristocracy, when Sicily was part of the Kingdom of Two Sicilies and controlled by the Bourbons. It's not the lightest read—dense musings about love, life, war, politics, family, religion, and death, all cleverly masking the simple story of a man and his dog, but if you can get past the first 25 pages, you won't put it down.

The restaurant bases its menu on the cuisine from The Kingdom of Two Sicilies (Southern Italy and Sicily). Chef Vito Gnazzo, from Salerno, oversees the kitchen from which he makes my favorite *spaghetti con bottarga di muggine* (the cured roe pouch of gray mullet). I love it! And the book and the restaurant. His version is better than mine, but you'll get the idea.

Serves 4–6

- ½ teaspoon crushed red pepper
- 2 cloves garlic, thinly sliced
- ⅓ cup extra virgin olive oil
- 1 pound spaghetti
- ½ cup finely chopped flat-leaf parsley
- 6 ounces grated fresh grey mullet bottarga

Bring a large pot of salted water to boil.

In a large skillet over medium-low heat, sauté the red pepper and garlic in the olive oil until just fragrant—about 2 minutes. Remove from heat.

Cook the spaghetti until *al dente* (about 2 minutes less than the package directions), drain and add to the olive oil mixture over medium heat. Add the parsley and toss to combine. Add the grated bottarga; toss until it is well incorporated.

Serve immediately.

Notes: Grated and dried bottarga, in a jar, can be substituted if fresh is not available. Tuna bottarga can also be used. You can find either at a specialty market or online.

VINO
Bianco: Sicilian Blends
Rosso: Nero d'Avola

Crisp whites and light reds with significant minerality work best with a salty, roe-focused dish. Ban tannin and forbid new oak. Welcome acidity! Sicilian white varieties tend to have fruit-neutral aromatics focused on scents like straw, beeswax and almonds and work well with the bottarga. Nero d'Avola can show very soft tannins. It offers a generous fruit core that washes away the saltiness the bottarga can build up.

FUSILLI CON BROCCOLI, ACCIUGHE E PINOLI

Fusilli with Broccoli, Anchovies, and Pine Nuts

When I think of Philadelphia, I think of Rocky Balboa punching carcasses in a meat locker. I think of cheese steaks. I think of South Philly's take on Italian cuisine: red sauce joints with names like Ralph's, serving big portions on checkered tablecloths. I conjure up this image not to disturb you, but so that you can now imagine its polar opposite.

The scene is Giacomo Bistrot in Milan. Forty or so seats, where the only things checkered come from Ferragamo and Gucci, and where the groomed and the manicured couldn't even imagine eating veal parmigiana with a side of mushy spaghetti, much less consider it to be Italian.

There, I recently ate a version of the following recipe. The pasta itself was called "fusilloro," which is fusilli with "oro" (for gold) at the end because they are extruded through a gold die, rather than the standard copper. This place, I promise you, is where the real 0.0001% eat. I can hear it now, "Yo, Adrian. What's for dinner?" "Hey, Rocky, let's get some fusilli at Giacomo." Or not …

Serves 4–6

¼ cup pine nuts

1 onion, finely chopped

¼ cup olive oil

4 stalks broccoli, florets only, rinsed

2 cups vegetable broth

Salt to taste

Freshly ground black pepper to taste

1 pound fusilli or cavatelli

10–12 oil-packed anchovies, each one cut into thirds

Grated Parmigiano

Bring a large pot of salted water to boil.

In a small skillet over medium heat, toast the pine nuts for a couple of minutes until golden. Remove from heat and set aside.

In a large skillet over medium heat, sauté the onion in olive oil until golden. Add the broccoli and mix together for a couple of minutes. Add the vegetable broth and cover. After 2–3 minutes, remove about half the broccoli and set aside. Cover the remaining broccoli and cook for 2–3 more minutes until soft. Use a hand-held blender to purée the broccoli and broth mixture until smooth. Add salt and pepper to taste.

Cook the pasta until *al dente* (about 2 minutes less than the package directions), drain and retain 1 cup of the cooking water. Add the pasta to the pot containing the broccoli puree and mix thoroughly. Add the broccoli florets, the anchovies and most of the pine nuts. Add some of the retained cooking water if it seems too dry.

Serve with the remaining pine nuts and grated Parmigiano.

VINO

Frizzante and Bianco: Sardinian Blends

Rosso: Sardinian Blends

Broccoli's green flavor, from a molecule called acetoin, frequently trips-up wine matches, and anchovies' umami and salty character can clash with wine, which contains no salt. Savory white wines with less overt fruit, like many from Sardinia, can do the work. The red berry fruits of Cannonau, Monica di Sardegna and Carignano di Sulcis contrast the pasta's savoriness while providing juiciness to buffer the anchovies' saltiness and broccoli's bitter bite.

BUCATINI ALL'AMATRICIANA
Bucatini with Pancetta, Tomato, and Onion

Would you ever eat lobster without wearing a bib? Only at your shirt's peril. But lobster is not alone. Although I can think of few bowls of anything that I like more than *bucatini all'amatriciana*, I find no food to be more bib-worthy. I've never escaped without wearing some of the accompanying sauce on my shirt. Why? Because bucatini is one thick string, and nearly impossible to twirl onto a fork without a little splash. I have found hope, however, in a recent discovery: three foot long bucatini. After the shock and awe wore off, I realized that the incredible length allowed for easy twirling with minimal splashing. So get it if you can. If not, break out the bib and enjoy.

Bucatini all'amatriciana is a favorite in Rome, but it hails from the mountain town of Amatrice in northern Lazio. There, purists would not substitute pancetta for guanciale. Nor would they add onion, though they might add a little chili pepper. The sauce is most often served with bucatini, but spaghetti or rigatoni will do.

Serves 4–6

6 ounces guanciale or pancetta
¼ cup olive oil
3 onions, thinly sliced
1 28-ounce can of peeled plum tomatoes, puréed
1 teaspoon salt
1 teaspoon freshly ground black pepper
½ teaspoon crushed red pepper—optional
1 pound bucatini or thick spaghetti
Grated Pecorino Romano cheese

Bring a large pot of salted water to a boil.

Cut the pancetta into ½ inch strips or small cubes.

In a large skillet, over medium heat, cook the pancetta in the olive oil for a minute. Add the onions. When the onion and pancetta are golden, add the tomatoes, salt and pepper—and if using, crushed red pepper. Cook for about 30 minutes, or until the sauce has reduced.

Cook the bucatini until *al dente* (about 2 minutes less than the package directions), drain, and add it to the skillet with the sauce. Cook together for one minute.

Serve with grated Pecorino.

Note: In Rome, guanciale is often used, but I prefer the meatier pancetta.

VINO
Rosso: Sangiovese

Guanciale and tomato dominate this dish by dynamically contrasting each other. The first is savory and fatty; the second is sweet-tart and acid. This is truly a dish for a mid-weight wine with crunchy red fruits to match the tomatoes and with enough pronounced acid and tannin to cut through the guanciale. Sangiovese (100% or blends) is a clear go-to for this dish because it possesses racy acidity and tart cherry flavors to match the tomatoes.

RISOTTO BASICS

Making risotto takes plenty of patience, as you have to add liquid at intervals throughout the entire cooking process. But when prepared properly, it will reward you with perfect creaminess, and a firm core to each delicate, fluffy grain of rice.

Italian rice can be grouped into four categories based on size and cooking time:

Commune/originario (Common)—This is the first strain found in Italy. Balilla, a version of common rice, is used for broths, puddings, fritters, and desserts as it is softer and has a smoother texture to it.

Semifino (Semifine)—One type of semifino rice is vialone nano which is known for its speedy cooking time. When cooked, semifino grains of rice are soft on the outside with a firm interior. This type is used best in molded dishes or the popular antipasto arancini.

Fino (Fine)—This third type of rice is good for boiling and risotto. It has a shorter cooking time. Popular varieties are S. Andrea, Roma, Europa.

Superfino (Superfine)—This rice is shorter in length and best by far for making risotto. The well-known Arborio and Carnaroli are perfect with their sticky and firm nature. Their longer cooking times allow for a creamier risotto.

About Risotto

Pasta invaded Italy from the South to the North, but risotto invaded from North to South. For this reason, risotto may be an even more popular first course, "primo," in the areas above the Po River, which provides the perfect geography for rice cultivation. With significant rice output in the Lombardy, Piedmont, and Veneto regions, Italy has become Europe's leading rice producer. Although rice was cultivated in India as early as 4000 BC, it is not known for certain how rice made its way to Italy, but we do know that in September of 1475, the Duke of Milan, Galeazzo Maria Sforza, promised 12 sacks of rice seeds to the Duke of Ferrara. Since that time, risotto has been cooked with almost as many different ingredients as has pasta, from meat to seafood, vegetable to dairy. The most classic preparation, of course, is that of Risotto all Milanese.

RISOTTO ALLA MILANESE DUE MODI
Risotto Milanese Two Ways

Waking up is easy in Italy. No hangovers. No "what have I done" moments. No unattractive surprises. This has nothing to do with excellent wine, superior genes, or meticulous grooming habits. No, it's easy to wake up in Italy because Italians know that they must face last night's choices in the morning, and so they show discipline and patience, and always wake up feeling healthy and proud.

Then they saunter over to the refrigerator and open it, knowing they'll still be madly in love with the leftovers from last night's delicious dinner. They understand that, as a rule, if it isn't really good at night, then it will be scary in the morning.

Yes! Last night's pasta, reheated in a pan with olive oil, may actually be even tastier than the original—and in my house, worth hiding in a corner of the refrigerator. The same is true for *Risotto alla Milanese*, which is always delicious when piping hot and freshly made, but may be even better when the leftovers are prepared *al salto*, or fried into a crispy cake. So delicious, in fact, that you'd be proud to introduce it to your family and friends.

Serves 4–6

- 2 0.0125 gram packets of ground saffron
- 4 cups beef or chicken stock, preferably homemade
- 1 onion, finely diced
- 6 tablespoons unsalted butter
- 3 tablespoons olive oil
- 1 cup Carnaroli or Arborio rice
- 1 cup dry white wine
- ½ cup freshly grated Parmigiano cheese, more for serving
- Salt to taste
- Freshly ground black pepper to taste

In a saucepan, over low heat, add the saffron to the stock and keep it warm.

In a large skillet, over medium heat, sauté the onion in 3 tablespoons of the butter and the olive oil until the onion is translucent. Add the rice and stir together until it's lightly toasted and opaque. Add the wine and let cook for a minute, then add a ladleful of the hot stock. Continue to cook and stir until the liquid is almost fully absorbed. Add a teaspoon of salt. As the liquid absorbs, add more stock, a ladleful at a time, waiting until it's almost completely absorbed before adding more. Cook until rice is al dente, about 15–18 minutes. Be careful not to overcook the rice. Remove the skillet from the heat and add the rest of the butter and the Parmigiano. Serve immediately

To prepare *al salto:* If using freshly made risotto, spread it on wax paper to cool it down. Divide risotto into equal portions of about 1 cup each. In a large skillet, preferably non-stick, over medium heat melt 1 tablespoon of butter and lower the heat. Place a portion of the risotto in the center of the pan. Use a spatula to flatten it into a circle. Cook for 3–5 minutes. Place a dinner plate over the top of the skillet and flip the risotto onto it and then slide it back into the skillet and cook for another 3–5 minutes. It should be golden brown on both sides. Repeat for additional cakes. Serve immediately.

Note: this takes some practice—keeping the risotto from breaking apart depends on your pan and stove. It's also possible to make a single, thicker cake by cooking all of the risotto together in a larger pan, and then cut into wedges to serve.

VINO
Bianco: Pinot Bianco
Rosso: Nebbiolo

A sumptuous risotto needs a wine with super-fresh acidity to keep the palate revived. This is especially true for whites, as most reds will have enough tannic thrust to pull the rice's richness right off the palate. Pinot Bianco and Nebbiolo are excellent options, not only for their pronounced acidity but also their flavors. Pinot Bianco is a good partner because of its subtle yellow apple and straw flavors, while Nebbiolo is fragrant with rose and spice notes.

SUNDAY PASTA

TABELLA DELLA PASTA
Table of Pasta

Name	Translation	Description	Region
Pasta Corta *(Short Pasta)*			
Calamaretti	Little Squids	Small, ring-shaped	Campania
Cannolicchi Rigati	Little Tubes	Hollow, tubular	Campania
Casarecce	Home-made	S-shaped	Sicily
Cavatappi	Corkscrews	Hollow	
Cavatelli	Often made with ricotta	Small, curved shape	Southern Italy
Conchiglie Rigate	Grooved shells	Shell-shaped	Campania
Creste di Galli	Coxcombs	With a crest.	Naples
Ditali Rigati	Grooved thimbles	Small stocky	Campania
Farfalle	Butterflies	Bowtie-shaped	Lombardy
Faralloni	Large Butterflies	Large version of farfalle	Lombardy
Fiocchi Rigati	Grooved flakes	Smaller version of farfalle with corrugated edges	
Fisarmoniche	Accordion	Accordion-shaped	Marche
Fusilli	Little spindles	Corkscrew-shaped	Molise
Garganelli	Gullet of a chicken	Similar to penne, but with a visible flap	Bologna
Gemelli	Twins	A single strand twisted in a spiral	
Gigli	Lilies	Small, cone-shaped	
Gramigna	Little weed	Short, thin, curled strand	Emilia-Romagna
Maccheroni		Short tubes (like ziti) (Also a generic term)	
Maltagliati	Badly Cut	Flat, diamond—shaped	
Manicotti	Sleeves	crepes which are folded around ricotta filling	
Mezze Ziti	Half Ziti	Smaller ziti	
Orecchiette	Little ears	Ear-shaped	Puglia
Paccheri	Slap		Campania
Penne	Quills	Tubular pasta pens.	
Penne Rigate	Grooved quills		Campania
Pennette		Shorter penne	
Pennoni		Longer penne	
Pipette	Little pipes	Small pipe-shaped	
Radiatori	Radiators	Small andwide with ruffled edges	
Riccioli	Curls	Curled, with a ribbed exterior	Emilia-Romagna
Rigatoncello		Narrow rigatoni	

Rigatoni	Large ridges	Tube shaped, larger than penne	Southern Italy
Rotelle, Ruote	Small wheels	Resembles small wheels	
Sagnarelli		Short, ribbon-shaped	Abruzzo
Spaccatelle		Short, tube-shaped	Sicily
Spirali	Spirals	Similar to, but slightly larger than cavatappi	
Stivaletti	Little boots	Small, curved tubes	
Strangolapreti		Thin, curly	
Strozzapreti (Strangozzi)	Priest stranglers	Similar to cavatelli, but longer.	Emilia-Romagna
Torchietti	Tiny torches	Small, bell-shaped	
Tortiglioni	Twists	Tubular, with pronounced grooves	Campania
Trenne		Similar to penne, but with a triangular cross-section	
Trofie		Short, twisted pasta	Liguria
Tubetti Rigati	Grooved tubes	Short, grooved, tubular	Campania
Pasta Lunga *(Long Pasta)*			
Bavette		Narrow version of tagliatelle	Genoa
Bucatini	Pierced	Thick, spaghetti-like	Abruzzo
Capellini	Fine hair	Extremely fine spaghetti	Lombardy
Colonne Pompeii		Longer fusilli	Campania
Fettuccine	Little ribbons	Long, flat	Lazio
Lasagna		Wide, flat	Emilia-Romagna
Linguine	Little tongues	Thin, flat	Liguria
Maccheroni alla Chitarra	From a guitar	Named for the tool used to make it—like strings on a guitar	Abruzzo
Mafaldine		Thin, rippled	
Pappardelle		Wide, flat, similar to fettuccine, but broader	Piedmont
Perciatelli		Thick, hollow pasta	
Perciatellini		Thinner perciatell.	
Scialatielli	To dishevel	Rustic pasta similar to fettuccine and tagliatelle	Naples
Spaghetti	Small strings	Long, thin pasta	
Spaghettini		Thinner spaghetti (not as thin as vermicelli).	
Tagliatelle	To cut	Long, flat, ribbon-shaped	Emilia-Romagna
Taglierini		Thinner version of tagliatelle	Piedmont
Tagliolini		Thinner version of tagliatelle	Emelia-Romagna
Tonnarelli		Long, square handmade spaghetti	
Trenette		Flat, narrow pasta	Liguria
Tripoline		Ribbon shaped, with only one curled edge	Southern Italy
Vermicelli	Little worms	Thinner spaghetti	Rome
Ziti	Grooms or brides	Tubular pasta	Sicily

Pasta Ripiena *(Filled Pasta)*			
Agnolotti	'Angelot' from Montferrat	Shell-shaped ravioli	Piedmont, Naples
Anolini		Small *ravioli*, usually beef	Emilia-Romagna
Cappelletti	Little hats	Parcels filled with meat and/or cheese	Emilia-Romagna
Cannelloni		Tubes, similar to **manicotti**, filled with meat and cheese	
Conchiglioni Rigati	Large ribbed shells	Large, shell-shaped	
Fagottini	Little purses	Pouch-shaped, filled with ricotta, similar to ravioli	
Lumaconi Rigati	Big ribbed snails	Snail-shaped	Campania
Pansotti	Pot-bellied	Ball-shaped	Puglia
Quadretti		Small, square, made with eggs	
Ravioli Quadrati	Square ravioli	Square ravioli	
Ravioli Tondi	Round ravioli	Round ravioli	
Raviolo	(pl) Ravioli	Two layers of dough, sealed around meat or cheese filling	
Tortelli		Filled rectangles, twisted at the ends into rings	
Tortellini		Smaller verion	Emilia
Tortelloni		Larger version	
Pasta Piccola *(Small Pasta)*			
Acini di Pepe	Peppercorns	Actually, smaller than peppercorns	
Anellini	Small rings	Ring-shaped	
Conchigliette Lisce	Small smooth shells	Shell-shap	Campania
Corallini Lisci	Small smooth coral	Jewel-shaped.	
Cuoretti	Tiny hearts	heart-shaped	
Farfalline	Tiny butterflies	Smaller version of farfalle	Lombardy
Funghini	Little mushrooms	Mushroom-shaped	
Lancette	Hands of a clock	Spear-shaped	
Orzo	Barley	Rice-shaped	Abruzzo
Pastina	Little pasta	Generic term for small pasta	
Puntalette	Tiny tips	rice-shaped	
Stelline	Little stars	star-shaped, with a center hole	
Stellette	Stars	Bigger stars	
Gnocchi *(Dumplings)*			
Gnocchetti Sardi	Sardinian dumplings	Another name for Malloreddus	Sardinia
Gnocchi	Dumplings	Shell-shaped dumpling, most often potato-based	Rome
Gnudi	Naked	Ricotta or spinach gnocchi	Tuscany
Malloreddus	Little bulls	Ridged, conch-shaped	Sardinia

GLOSSARIO

Glossary

A

Acciuga; pl. acciughe—Anchovy, Anchovies from the Mediterranean.

Aceto balsamico—Balsamic vinegar.

Acido—Sour, acidic, or tart.

Acqua—Water.

Acqua Minerale—Mineral water.
    Gassata or frizzante—Sparkling.
    Naturale—Still.

Affettati—Cold cuts; cut in slices.

Affumicato—Smoked.

Aglio—Garlic.

Al dente—"To the tooth." The texture of firm cooked pasta.

Al forno—Baked in an oven.

Al fresco—To dine outdoors.

Alcool—General term for alcohol, potable or otherwise. It is usually stated by percent of volume.

Alici,—Anchovy.

Alimentare—A general term referring to food, i.e. negozio alimentare, grocery store.

Alloro, foglia di—Bay leaf.

Amaro—Bitter; general term for "bitter" drinks.

Annata—Year; vintage for wine.

Antipasto—Appetizer, appetizer course; served before the Primo, or pasta course:

Aperitivo—Aperitif.

Appassire—To sauté or lightly fry.

Appiattire—The act of flattening meat with a kitchen mallet.

Apribottiglie—Bottle opener (not a corkscrew).

Aromi—Herbs.

Asiago—Sharp cow's milk cheese.

Asparagi—Asparagus.

Assaggio—Taste or sample.

Assortito—Assorted or varied.

Azienda Agricola—Farming business. A farm or estate which produces all or most of the grapes for wine sold under its labels.

B

Baggiano—Fava beans.

Bagnomaria—Double boiler or saucepan.

Balsamico—Balsamic vinegar.

Bar—Café or coffee shop.

Barbabietola—Beet.

Basilico—Basil.

Ben cotto—Well done or well-cooked.

Bere—To drink.

Bevanda—Beverage or drink.

Bibita—Beverage. Usually non-alcoholic.

Bicchiere—Drinking glass.

Bietola—Swiss chard.

Bistecca—Beef steak (though the term also applies to a veal or pork chop).

Bocconcino—Small, "bite-sized" mozzarella cheese balls.

Bollicine—Bubbles.

Bollito—Boiled.

Bottarga—Dried roe sac of gray mullet or tuna. It is sliced very thin or grated and used in salads and on pasta.

Botte—Barrel, cask, keg; the amount of liquid held in one of these objects, a unit of measurement.

Bottega—Shop or store.

Bottiglia—Bottle.

Braciola—Chop or steak.

Bresaola—Air-dried beef.

Broccolo—Broccoli, also broccoletti.

Brodo—Broth or stock.

Bruschetta—Diced tomatoes and garlic on toasted bread, drizzled with olive oil.

Brut—Dry sparkling wine.

Buco—"Hole" or "small space." A term is used in Tuscany to refer to a typical cellar *trattoria*.

Bufalo—Water Buffalo.
    Mozzarella di bufala—cheese made from the milk of water buffalo.

Buon appetito—"Good appetite." A salutation used to begin a meal.

Burrata—Made from mozzarella and cream. This cheese has a [semi-soft outer shell and a soft inside.

Burro—Butter.

C

Cacio—A specific type of cheese. Also, a general term for cheese, used in Central and Southern Italy.

Cacio e pepe—Spaghetti with *Pecorino Romano* cheese and black pepper. A Roman specialty.

Caciocavallo—"Horse cheese." A firm buffalo or cow's milk cheese, named for its resemblance to saddlebags.

Caciotta—Soft, fresh ewe's milk whey cheese from Campania.

Caffe'—Coffee.

Calamaro—Squid. Squid ink is often used as a coloring and flavoring agent for pastas, *risotto*, and other dishes.

Caldo—Hot.

Calice—Stem glass.

Calza—Cheesecloth.

Cameriere—Waiter.

Cameriera—Maid, waitress.

Cannella—Cinnamon.

Cantina—Wine cellar or winery.

Caponata—Sicilian vegetable dish made with eggplant, tomatoes, peppers, chili peppers, vinegar and onions.

Capperi—Capers, both brined and fresh.

Cappesante—Scallop.

Cappuccino—*Espresso* topped with foamed, steamed milk.

Caprese, alla—"Capri-style." Refers to a lightly cooked sauce of tomatoes, basil, olive oil and *mozzarella*.

Capricciosa, alla—"Capricious style." Referring to any dish prepared at the whimsy of the cook.

Caprino—Fresh goat's cheese.

Carbonara, alla—Sauce made from beaten eggs, grana, *Pecorino*, and *pancetta*.

Carciofo—Artichoke.

Carciofini—Small artichokes or artichoke hearts. Often marinated in olive oil.

Carne—Meat.

Carote—Carrots.

Casa vinicola—Wine house or merchant (**commerciante**) whose wine comes mainly from purchased grapes [or wines.]?

Casa, della—A specialty of a restaurant, may be either food or wine.

Casalinga, alla—"Housewife style." Also **alla casereccia**. Any dish cooked in a homey style or homemade.

Cascina—Farmhouse, often used for estate.

Castelmagno—Sharp, blue-veined, cow's milk cheese named after the town where it is produced in Piedmont.

Cavolfiore—Cauliflower.

Cavolini di Bruxelles—Brussels sprouts.

Cavolo—Cabbage.

Ceci—Chickpeas (garbanzo beans).

Cefalo—Grey mullet.

Cena—Dinner.

Cereali—General term for grains.

Chiocciole—Snails.

Chitara, alla—"Guitar style." Fresh egg pasta typical of Abruzzo, so named because it's made by pushing pasta sheets through a stringed tool that resembles a guitar).

Ciabatta—"Slipper." A slipper-shaped bread with a characteristically airy texture.

Cibo—Food.

Cicoria—Chicory.

Cime di rapa—Turnip greens, usually boiled and seasoned.

Cinghiale—Wild boar.

Cioccolata—Chocolate.

Cipolla—Onion.

Classico—Historic core of a DOC wine production zone.

Cocciola—Cockle.

Colapasta—Colander.

Colazione—Breakfast.

Coltello—Knife.

Comino—Cumin. [Used as a ground spice for stews and desserts.]

Conchiglie—Generic term for hard-shelled mollusks (clams, mussels, scallops, etc.).

Condimenti—Condiments.

Confetteria—Sweet confection.

Coniglio—Rabbit.

Consorzio—Consortium of producers.

Conto—Restaurant bill.

Contorno—Side dish or garnish to complement the main course.

Coppa—Pressed, cooked, boneless pork neck. Also called **capocollo** in Southern Italy.

Coriandolo—Coriander.

Cosciotto—Leg of meat.

Costa—Chop of meat.

Costata—Rib steak of beef or veal

Costoletta—Chop; cutlet; rib.

Cotoletta—Cutlet (veal unless otherwise specified) usually breaded and fried.

Cotto—Cooked.

Cozze—Mussels. Also called **mitili, muscioli, muscoli, and peoci**.

Crema—Cream.

Crespelle—Crêpes.

Crostacei—General term for crustaceans, such as shrimp, lobster, crabs.

Crostini—Toasted bread, usually with a savory topping.

Crudo—Raw; uncooked.

Cucchiaio—Spoon.

Cucina—Kitchen; stove.

Culatello—Cured pork rump, sliced and eaten as an *antipasto*.

Cuoco—Cook.

D

Diavola, alla—"Devil's style" or "devilled." Refers to spicy dishes.

Diavolillo (Diavolicchio)—"Little devil." Abruzzese name for fresh or dried chili pepper.

Digestivo—An after dinner digestive drink such as *grappa*, or an herbal liqueur such as *amaro*.

Dolce—Sweet.

Dolcelatte—A blue-veined, soft, creamy cheese, named "sweetmilk" for the flavor.

Dorato—Referring to food that is golden in color or gilded. Often something dipped in egg and fried until golden brown.

Dragoncello—Tarragon.

E

Emiliano—Emilian granular cheese.

Emmentaler—Like Swiss cheese, a cow's milk cheese commonly used in pasta dishes, polenta, and on pizza.

Enologo—Enologist with a university degree; **enotecnico** is a winemaking technician with a diploma.

Enoteca—Wine bar

Erba cipollina—Chives.

Erbe—Herbs; **erbe aromatiche** are scented types, such as basil, rosemary, sage, thyme and parsley; **erbe selvatiche** are wild.

Erbe fini—A mixture of chopped herbs used as a flavoring for stocks and stews.

Espresso—Highly concentrated cup of coffee made from roasted Arabica beans forced through a pressure valve or with a drip pot.

Estratto—Extract (often lemon or vanilla)

Estratto di Pomodoro—Tomato paste

Etichetta—Label.

Ettaro—Hectare (2 471 acres). The standard measure of vineyard surface in Italy.

Etto—Standard unit of 100 grams.

Ettolitro—Hectoliter or 100 liters. The standard measure of wine volume in Italy.

F

Fagiolo—Bean.

Fagiolini—String beans.

Fame—Hunger.

Far sudare—To braise.

Farina—Flour.

Farinacei—General term for starch foods.

Farro—Spelt.

Fattoria—Farm or estate.

Fave—Fava beans.

Fecola—Starch, usually from potato (or cornstarch).

Filetto—Tenderloin; filet mignon.

Finocchio—Fennel.

Finnocchiona—Tuscan salami seasoned with fennel seeds, salt, pepper, and garlic.

Fiore—Flower; **fiori di zucca** or **zucchini** squash flowers, usually stuffed and fried.

Fior di latte—Cow's milk *Mozzarella*.

Fiorentina, alla—"Florentine style," usually referring to a dish made with spinach.

Focaccia—Puffy yeast bread baked in a pan.

Focolare—An open hearth or fireplace used for cooking.

Fonduta—Cheese fondue.

Fontana—A mound of flour with a well in it to absorb liquid and eggs.

Fontina—Soft unpasteurized cow's milk cheese from Valle d'Aosta.

Forchetta—Fork.

Formaggio—Cheese.

Fornaio—Baker.

Forno—Oven; baker's shop.

Fragola—Strawberry.

Fragolino—Pandora fish. A sea bream that is good baked, grilled or fried.

Frantoio—Mill where olives are processed into oil. Also, olive press.

Frasca—Friulian term for a restaurant located near a winery.

Freddo—Cold.

Fresco—Fresh.

Friarelli—Broccoli rabe in Naples.

Friggere—To fry.

Fritto—Fried. **Fritto misto** is a "mixed fry" of battered or breaded vegetables, meat or seafood.

Frizzante—Fizzy or faintly fizzy (wine) or mineral water.

Frutta—Fruit.

Frutti di bosco—Berries.

Fumetto—Concentrated chicken or beef broth.

Funghi—Mushrooms.

Fuori stagione—Out of season.

Fuso—Melted (butter).

G

Gambero—Crustaceans. **Gambero rosso** and **gambero imperiale** or **mazzancolla** are large Mediterranean prawns, also called **gamberoni**; **gamberelli** are smaller prawns; **gamberetti** tiny shrimp; **gamberi d'acqua dolce** freshwater crayfish.

Gassato, gasato—Carbonated; sparkling.

Gastronomia—Gastronomy. Can also refer to a gourmet food or specialty store.

Gazzosa—Lemon-flavored carbonated water.

Gelato—Italian ice cream.

Ghiaccio—Ice or ice cubes.

Gianduja—Piedmontese chocolate and hazelnut paste.

Giardiniera, alla—Dishes prepared "garden style"—with chopped vegetables and salad greens.

Giorno, del—A restaurant's daily special.

Girarrosto—Roasted on a spit.

Gorgonzola—Strong, Lombardian, blue-veined, cow's milk cheese, made in and around the town of Gorgonzola.

Grana—The grainy texture of certain Italian cheeses. Used colloquially to refer to Parmigiano-Reggiano or Grana Padano.

Grana Padano—A granular Italian cheese, aged 1 year to 18 months, which dates back to the twelfth century.

Grano—Grain; wheat.

Grano saraceno—Buckwheat flour; used to prepare polenta and pasta.

Grappa—Spirit distilled from grapes previously crushed for wine.

Grasso—Fat (including animal fats like lard and suet).

Guanciale—Salt pork from the cheek or jowl, used as a flavoring in soups, stews, pastas and other dishes.

Guarnito—Garnished.

Gusto—Flavor; taste.

I

Imbottigliata—Bottled (**all'origine** implies at the source).

Impanare—To coat or roll in breadcrumbs.

Impanato—Breaded.

Impastare—To knead.

Indivia—Endive.

Invidia riccia/Scaroloa—curly leaf escarole

Invidia belga/Insalata belga—Belgian endive

Insaccato—A general term for salami and sausages.

Insalata—Salad.

Integrale—Whole wheat.

Invecchiato—Aged or cured.

Involtini—Thin slices of meat, such as veal, pork or fish, which are rolled and stuffed.

K

Kasher—Kosher.

L

Lardo—Lard: the layer of fat directly under a pig's skin.

Latte—Milk; **latticini**: dairy products.

Lattuga—Lettuce.

Lauro—Bay leaf.

Legno—Wood.

Legume—Legumes.

Lenticchie—Lentils.

Lesso—Boiled.

Limone—Lemon; limonata lemonade; limetta or limone bergamotto lime, limoncello lemon liqueur.

Liquori—Liqueurs. Refers to distilled spirits, such as *grappa* and brandy, as well as compositions, such as *amaro*, *limoncello* and *sambuca*.

Lista del vivande—Menu of a restaurant. Also **menú**, more commonly used.

Litro—Liter.

Locanda—Inn. Synonymous with **osteria** or **trattoria** (see).

M

Maccheroni—Macaroni; a generic term for dried pasta in Southern Italy, though elsewhere it refers to short pasta tubes like *rigatoni* and *ziti*.

Macelleria—Butcher shop, **macellaio** butcher.

Macinapepe—Pepper mill.

Macinare—To grind; mince.

Maggiorana—Marjoram.

Magro—Lean, as in *carne magra*, lean meat.

Maiale—Pork.

Mais—Corn, sweet corn; maize.

Mandolino—Slicing multi-blade utensil for vegetable.

Mandorle—Almonds.

Mantecato—Ingredients pounded into a paste. Also, a general term referring to the technique of sautéeing pasta in a skillet with some of its sauce and grana. It's also the term used in Northern Italy, (esp. Veneto) of adding butter to a dish to finish it, (esp. risotto—risotto mantecato).

Manzo—Beef.

Marinata—Marinade.

Marrone—Chestnut.

Mascarpone—A fresh, soft cream cheese, similar to butter. Unsweetened, it can be used in pasta or *risotto*. Sweetened, it is served in desserts, such as *Tiramisu*.

Mattarello—Rolling pin.

Medaglione—"Medallion." A thick cut of meat or fish.

Melanzane—Eggplant.

Menta—Mint.

Mercato—Market.

Merenda—Snack, light meal or picnic, also called **spuntino**.

Metodo Charmat—Sparkling wine made using the sealed tank method.

Metodo Classico—Sparkling wine made using the bottle fermentation method.

Mezzaluna—Curved chopping knife with two handles.

Miele—Honey.

Milanese, alla—"Milan style." Dishes associated with Milan

Minestra—Generic term for soup. Also used for *first course*.

Minestra in brodo—Broth with pasta or rice; **minestrone** is hearty vegetable soup; **Minestrina** is a light soup or broth; see also **zuppa**.

Misticanza—Salad of wild greens like arugula, endive and watercress.

Mitili—Mussels, also called **cozze**.

Mollica di Pane—Breadcrumb. (The mollica is the soft, inside of the bread.)

Moscato—Nutmeg.

Mosciame—Dried, salted strips of dolphin, swordfish or tuna.

Mosto del Vino—Wine must.

Mozzarella—Smooth, soft, white cheese originally from the milk of water buffalo (*di bufala*), mozzarella **fior di latte** is made from cow's milk

Muggine—Gray mullet. Usually grilled.

Mustica—Hot sauce made from dried anchovy or sardine, chili peppers and olive oil.

N

Napoletana, alla—"Neapolitan style." Any of a variety of dishes associated with Naples.

Nocciola—Hazelnut. The most widely used nut in Italian cooking.

Noci—Nuts; walnuts.

Nonna, della—"Grandma style." Any dish prepared according to a home-style cooking tradition.

Norma, alla'—Sicilian *pasta* dish with tomato, fried eggplant and grated salted *ricotta*.

O

Olio extra vergine d'oliva– Extra virgin olive oil.

Ombra—Shade. A small glass of white wine, esp. in Venice.

Orzo—Barley.

P

Paglia e fieno—Literally "hay and straw." Green and yellow pasta strands.

Pancetta—Taken from the belly or cheek of a pig. Consists of layers of fat and lean tissue.

Pangrattato—Dry breadcrumbs.

Parmigiana, alla—Parma-style (not necessarily made with Parmigiano).

Passata di pomodoro—Tomato purée (generally sold in bottles).

Pastinaca—Parsnip.

Pecorino—Sheep's milk cheese.

Pepe verde—Green peppercorns.

Pepe—Black pepper.

Peperoncino—Crushed red pepper.

Peperoni—Sweet (Bell) peppers

Pesce—Fish.
Pesto—Ligurian (pasta) sauce made with fresh basil, pine nuts, Pecorino, and olive oil.
Piadina—Round, flat bread. From Romagna.
Piccante—Hot; spicy.
Piselli—Peas.
Polenta—A thick porridge, typically made from cornmeal.
Pollame—Poultry.
Pollo—Chicken; fowl.
Polpette—Meatballs.
Polpo—Octopus.
Pomodoro—Tomato.
Porchetta—Roasted pork stuffed with salt, black pepper, wild fennel, and garlic.
Porco—Pig.
Porro—Leek.
Pranzo—Lunch.
Prezzemolo—Parsley.
Prosciutto di Parma—Dry-cured ham that is salted, and aged 10 to 12 months. Only produced within the province of Parma.
Prosciutto cotto—Cooked ham.
Prosciutto di San Daniele—Salty and sweet flavored ham with a smooth texture made with pigs bred in Northern Italy.
Provola—Buffalo or cow's milk cheese typical of southern Italy.
Prugna—Prune, plum.
Puttanesca, alla—"Whore's-style." A quick-cooked tomato sauce that also includes black olives, capers, anchovies, and red pepper.

Q

Q.B. (Quanto basta)—"As needed," or "to taste".

R

Rabarbaro—Rhubarb.
Rafano—Horseradish.
Ragu'—Sauce made with meat, tomato, onions, and other ingredients.

Rapini—*Broccoli di rape* (known in the United States as broccoli rabe).
Ricotta- *Fresh cheese*, made using the whey from sheep's milk.
Robiola—Soft cheese typical of Lombardy and Piedmont.
Rinforzo—"Reinforcement." Neapolitan pickled salad of cauliflower, olive and capers.
Risaia—Rice paddy.
Robiola—Mild and buttery cow's milk cheese.
Romana, alla—In the Roman style.
Romanello—Very hard, skim milk cheese. Mainly used for grating.
Rosmarino—Rosemary.
Roventino—Typical Tuscan blood sausage.
Rucola—Arugula.
Ruote—"Wheels." Wheel-shaped pasta.

S

Salto—Lightly-fried.
Salumeria—A shop that sells only cold cuts and cured meats.
Salvia—Sage (herb).
Salviata—Sage custard.
Sanguinaccio—Sweet pudding made from pig's blood and chocolate.
Sardina—Sardine.
Scalogna, scalogno—Shallot; green onion.
Scamorza—Pear-shaped cheese made with sheep's or cow's milk.
Scarpetta, fare la—Wiping one's plate with a piece of bread to soak up any remaining sauce. "To make the little shoe".
Segale—Rye.
Seppia—Cuttlefish. Similar to, but generally more tender than squid.
Soffritto—Combination of chopped carrots, onions, celery, and garlic that are slowly cooked in butter, olive oil, or lard. The starting point of many Italian dishes.
Sogliola—Sole.
Soppressata—A cured pork sausage

Speck—Smoked and cured boneless haunch of a pig.
Spezie—Spices.
Spigola—Sea bass.
Spinaci—(pl.) Spinach.
Spuntino—Snack.
Strapazzate—Uova; scrambled eggs.

T

Tagliata—Fine slices of rare beefsteak.
Timo—Thyme.
Tonno—Tuna.
Totano—Squid.
Triglia—Red mullet.
Troccoli—Rustic *tagliatelle*. Usually served with meat sauces.

U

Ubriaco—"Drunken." Refers to dishes that contain a large amount of alcohol.
Umbrici—Fat, handmade spaghetti from Umbria.
Unto—Oily, greasy.
Uovo—Egg
Uva—Grape.
Uvetta—Raisin.

V

Vaniglia—Vanilla.
Vin santo—Tuscan dessert wine. Has a nutty-caramel flavor and a deep golden color. **Vinello**—A light table wine.
Vitella—Veal.
Vongole—Clams.

Z

Zafferano—Saffron.
Zenzero—Ginger.
Zucca—Pumpkin or squash.
Zucchero—Sugar.
Zucchina/Zucchino—Zucchini or squash.

INDICE

Index

B
Basic Pasta Recipe 28

C
Cooking Pasta 27

F
Food Classification System 13
- DOP 13
- IGP 13
- STG 13

Formaggio (Cheese) 14
- Burrata 14, 90
- Fontina 14, 94, 126
- Gorgonzola 14, 94
- Grana Padano 14
- Mascarpone 14, 94, 108
- Mozzarella 14, 62, 76, 78, 90, 102, 110, 124, 136
- Parmigiano Reggiano 14, 15, 30, 34, 40, 48, 50, 58, 64, 66, 68, 70, 74, 76, 78, 82, 84, 90, 92, 94, 96, 98, 100, 102, 104, 106, 108, 110, 112, 114, 118, 120, 124, 126, 128, 130, 132, 136, 140, 146, 154, 155
- Pecorino 15, 36, 56, 130
- Provolone 15, 118, 126
- Ricotta 15, 34, 64, 80, 82, 108, 112, 124, 136, 149
- Ricotta Salata 15, 80

Frutta, Noci, e Miscellanea (Fruits, Nuts, and Miscellany)
- Acciughe. Alici. (Anchovies) 20, 140
- Brodo di Verdure (Vegetable Broth) 20, 50, 140
- Capperi (Capers) 20, 72, 134
- Farina (Flour) 20, 24, 25, 28, 82, 110, 112
- Limone (Lemon) 20, 44, 50, 74, 108
- Mandorla (Almond) 20, 52
- Noci (Walnuts) 20, 108
- Olio Extravergine (Extra Virgin Olive Oil) 21, 54, 62, 68, 72, 138
- Olio Virgine (Virgin Olive Oil) 21
- Olive e Olio d'Oliva (Olives and Olive Oil) 20
- Pepe (Pepper) 21, 29, 30, 34, 36, 38, 40, 44, 46, 48, 50, 52, 54, 56, 58, 62, 64, 66, 70, 72, 74, 76, 78, 80, 84, 86, 90, 92, 94, 96, 98, 100, 102, 104, 106, 110, 112, 114, 118, 120, 122, 124, 126, 128, 130, 132, 136, 138, 140, 142, 146
- Pinoli (Pine Nuts) 21, 52, 68, 104, 108, 140
- Pistacchio (Pistachio) 21, 46
- Sale (Salt) 21
- Sarde (Sardines) 21, 52

M
Methods of preparation 25
- Forme di Pasta (Pasta Shapes) 26
  - *Fettuce (Ribbons)* 26
  - *Forme Unici (Unique Shapes)* 26
  - *Micro Pasta (Tiny Shapes)* 26
  - *Pasta Lunga (Long Strands)* 26
  - *Ripieni (Filled)* 26
  - *Tubi Corti (Short tubes)* 26
  - *Tubi Lunghi (Long Tubes)* 26
- Pasta Artigianale (Artisanal Pasta) 26
- Pasta Fresca (Fresh Pasta) 25
- Pasta Ripiena (Filled Pasta) 26
- Pasta Secca (Dry Pasta) 25

P
Pasta Rules: The Do's and Don'ts 27

S
Salsa di Pomodoro (Tomato Sauce) 29, 66

Salumi (Cured Meats) 16
- Guanciale 16, 130, 142
- Pancetta 16, 36, 46, 70, 92, 100, 104, 118, 126, 130, 132, 142
- Prosciutto 16, 42, 46, 48, 62, 76, 84, 124, 132
- Salciccia 16
- Speck 16, 84

V
Verdure (Vegetables) 17
- Aglio (Garlic) 17, 50, 54, 56, 62, 64, 66, 68, 72, 96, 98, 100, 102, 106, 108, 114, 118, 120, 126, 132, 134, 138
- Asparagi (Asparagus) 17, 40, 44
- Basilico (Basil) 17, 30, 62, 66, 68, 78, 80, 112, 132, 136
- Broccoli 17, 56, 98, 140
- Carciofi (Artichokes) 17, 50
- Cavolfiore (Cauliflower) 17, 126
- Cavolini (Cavoletti) di Bruxelles (Brussels Sprouts) 17, 100
- Cipolla (Onion) 17, 29, 30, 36, 38, 40, 42, 44, 46, 48, 52, 70, 72, 76, 78, 80, 84, 90, 92, 104, 106, 112, 124, 128, 132, 136, 140, 142, 146
- Fagioli e Legumi (Beans and Legumes) 17, 106, 132
- Finocchio (Fennel) 18, 52, 96
- Melanzane (Eggplant) 18, 80
- Origano (Oregano) 18
- Peperoncino (Chili Pepper) 18, 56, 142
- Peperoni (Bell Peppers) 18, 102
- Piselli (Peas) 18, 48, 58, 92, 128
- Pomodori (Tomatoes) 18, 29, 30, 38, 42, 66, 72, 76, 78, 80, 112, 118, 122, 124, 128, 132, 134, 136, 142
- Porcini (Mushrooms) 19, 48, 104, 110, 120
- Prezzemolo (Parsley) 19, 29, 38, 40, 50, 62, 72, 78, 112, 114, 118, 120, 122, 132, 134, 136, 138
- Radicchio 19, 84
- Rapini (Broccoli Rabe) 19, 56
- Rosmarino (Rosemary) 19
- Salvia (Sage) 19, 34, 82, 132
- Spinaci (Spinach and Chard) 19, 28, 34, 82, 92, 102, 108
- Zucchine 19, 40, 70, 90

W
Wine Classification System 13
- DOC 13
- DOCG 13
- IGT 13
- Vino Da Tavola—Table Wine 13

Notes

Notes

www.Garrubbo.com